Presented To:

_____

From:

_____

Date:

_____

Encounters

Encounters

Stories of Healing

Randy Hill

DESTINY IMAGE₍₎ PUBLISHERS, INC.

P.O. Box 310, Shippensburg, PA 17257-0310

"Speaking to the Purposes of God for This Generation and for the Generations to Come."

This book and all other Destiny Image, Revival Press, MercyPlace, Fresh Bread, Destiny Image Fiction, and Treasure House books are available at Christian bookstores and distributors worldwide.

For a U.S. bookstore nearest you, call **1-800-722-6774.**

For more information on foreign distributors, call **717-532-3040.**

Reach us on the Internet: **www.destinyimage.com.**

ISBN 13 TP: 978-0-7684-3767-6

ISBN 13 Ebook: 978-0-7684-9000-8

For Worldwide Distribution, Printed in the U.S.A.

1 2 3 4 5 6 7 8 9 10 /15 14 13 12 11

Dedication

I want to dedicate this book to my father, Fred Lawson Hill who taught me…

…that the family is the first priority. I am to take care of them, that's my job!

…that my wife is the most important friend I have. No one else will be with me every day until I die. Invest in the future by caring for her now. Chances are she will have to take care of you some day.

…honesty and integrity are required values for any husband and father. If you say anything, speak the truth and make sure your handshake is as good as a contract.

…hard work is good for you!

…never be afraid to learn new skills; learn to do as many things as you possibly can and you will never be out of work.

…that Post Toasties are a good way to start the day and cornbread and beans are a full meal anytime.

…the value of a pickup truck and that the dashboard is an alternate storage place for everything including receipts, gloves, ice scrapers, and bailing wire.

…that anyone can dive with their legs straight…it takes real talent to dive like a frog.

…any job is an admirable job as long as it is moral, ethical, and legal. Its value is based on your excellence in performing the duties not in the opinion of others.

…faithfulness, showing up everyday, is essential for life. Even the overwhelming challenges of life can be conquered one day at a time, if you show up every day. You eat an elephant the same way you eat a banana…one bite at a time.

…that love is action not words only!

…if you keep looking over your shoulder for the approval of those watching, you will never plow a straight row.

…you teach more with your actions than with your words.

…a job is made easier with the right tools.

Many of these things you never said. Years ago, had someone asked what I learned from my Dad I might have said a few of these. However, now that I am older, I realize you were a great teacher. You said little but you modeled much. Thanks Dad for being the faithful man you were. If I have been successful, it can be traced to this heritage. I hope my children learn as much from me.

Thanks Dad!

Acknowledgments

Dana, you are my best friend, my lover, and the mother of my three favorite ladies in the world. Thank you for believing in me and always supporting the dream. You are my balance.

Anna, Ashley, and Alisha, you girls are more than a blessing to me. You have trained me well and there is no one who can wrap me around their finger like you can and I have found that to be a comfortable place. It's Friday night...

Mom, you have been the one behind the scenes praying me toward my destiny, my chief intercessor from birth. Thank you for being faithful in your call so I can fulfill mine.

Steve, you have always been my hero. You have spoken into my life on so many occasions that I cannot count them. You are a good brother and have been there through thick and thin always being the voice of reason with words like "They might beat you but they can't eat you" and "Hang in there like a hair in a biscuit". Thanks for always speaking straight with me.

Barbara, thank you for believing in your little brother and for your encouraging words after reading the original manuscript. I hope you like the edited version more.

Ray and Shirley, Oma and Opa, you adopted me as a son and have always believed in me. Thanks for raising the best daughter in the world and allowing her to be my wife.

Andrew and Amy, thanks for your help in transcribing and editing the verbal maze that was the beginning of *Encounters*. Your perspective and expertise helped so much.

Larry and Hutch, thanks for your friendship and encouragement as I pursued publication of this book. You guys have become friends for a lifetime giving me the push I need.

Sam and Beth, thanks for believing in me and hearing the voice of the Holy Spirit. May Jonathan's memory live on and accomplish his destiny in and through others.

Thank you Summit Church Family for loving us and helping us change the spiritual atmosphere over our county.

Dad, though you may have never read a full book during your life, you were the one that sparked the beginnings of this journey. I miss you.

Endorsements

Randy Hill has the uncommon ability to take words off the pages of history, getting inside a person and bringing that person to life. Time after time in trauma after trauma he brings broken, defeated, hopeless, helpless people to Jesus where they find wholeness. Bottom line for the reader: If He can do it for such as these, He can surely do it for me! May the reader see Jesus as they did and be made whole as they were.

Jack Taylor
President, Dimensions Ministries
Melbourne, Florida

Randy Hill has always been "after God's heart." As his pastor during his growing up years, I saw him come to classes, even as a youth, to learn more about our Lord. I am a Randy Hill fan! This book is a worthy read and comes from a godly man's heart. Best of all, he lives what he writes!

Morris Sheats, D.Min.
Founder/President, Leadership Institute
Founder/President, Heritage Church Dallas

Reading Randy Hill's book, *Encounters*, is like getting the original behind-the-scenes interview with the amazing people of the Bible, providing amazing insight into their thoughts and feelings. Even more, each unabridged dialogue, based on the scriptural account, has present day application, enabling the reader to readily identify with each character.

I love this book! I now feel like I intimately know the people I had previously only known from a distance in my past reading of the Bible. It's like going to Israel today and walking in the footsteps of Jesus as He would have traveled from town to town.

I will never read the Bible the same! It has become more alive, vibrant, and personal after reading *Encounters*! I hope Randy writes a sequel soon, revealing other characters of the Bible who made such a great contribution to our faith.

Kevin Dedmon
Author, *The Ultimate Treasure Hunt* and
Unlocking Heaven

Wow! Randy Hill has hit a home run with this book! You will be encouraged and touched deeply by Randy's ability to bring to life the stories of those who had life-changing encounters with Jesus. It will move you to believe in a fresh way. It will inspire hope for the hurting around you. It will ignite an awareness that God is still a miracle-working God. And it will stir a hunger in you to see Jesus like never before. I highly recommend *Encounters*.

Steve Backlund
Associate Pastor, Bethel Church
Global Legacy
Founder, Ignited Hope Ministries
Author, *Possessing Joy* and
You're Crazy If You Don't Talk To Yourself

Contents

Purpose

DOWN through the ages, there have been people in Scripture with the same dilemmas as people today. We have seen many perspectives of these situations, but rarely do we see them from the view of the person involved in the stories. What were their fears and doubts? What were their thoughts as the situations they found themselves in unfolded before their eyes? They were not unlike people today. We would ask many of the same questions if we were in their shoes. But what were those questions? I think we immortalize the people in the Bible as untouchable, special, not real people at all, and yet they were real. They were not chosen for examples because of their holiness or righteousness, but rather because they were just like you and me. That is what makes the Bible timeless. Its truth is as relevant today as it was 2000 years ago.

My purpose in writing this book is to show the human element of Scripture in the lives that Jesus touched personally. Those who saw Him first as the answer to their questions had many of the thoughts and questions that you and I have today. Though they took place in a totally different setting than modern day America, the stories of 2000 years ago become a little more relevant when we see the players in the stories as real people, not unlike us. I hope readers will be able to identify with many of the characters in the book and possibly even get a first time or new glimpse of the author and the finisher of our faith, Jesus. I know when they see Him for who He really is, they will be changed for eternity.

Introduction

WHAT could 2000-year-old stories have to do with my life today? I think it is an honest question that deserves an answer. What could be the relevance of stories so old? How could reading them be worth my time? What difference could they make? The answer may not be in the stories as much as in the one who wrote them—Jesus. Now, before you lay this book down and discount it as some religious ploy, take a moment and consider how the people in the following stories were not unlike you. Yes, they lived in a totally different time and place, but they had many of the problems we have today. How to make a living, how to succeed in their endeavors, how to make a marriage work, how to manage despite handicaps and disease—these are but a few of the things they dealt with just as we do today. How did they deal with them? What questions did they have, and what answers did they find? Could they be relevant in this millennium?

You have heard it said, "seeing is believing." We all have a little Missouri in us, don't we? You have probably said it or at least thought, "Show me and I will believe." The problem with that is our sight. We see things all the time, but our sight will not take us to the depths needed for understanding and comprehension. We see the trees sway in the breeze and say the wind is blowing, but where is it coming from and where is it going? The light of dawn tells us another day has begun. We see the day begin, but why does the sun continue to rise everyday as it has for millennia past without fail? I want us to gain a new perspective. We must change our perception and realize "seeing is believing" is an ill-advised life perspective. We must discover a new and living way: "Believing is seeing."

Now, I am not proposing some positive thinking, power of the mind hocus-pocus. No, I am speaking about a power beyond the human mind that will yield the truth of what we believe into reality in our lives. Each vignette presented in this book shows us a miracle that began with believing. Each of these people believed what they needed was present in the person Jesus Christ. Not in His Church, not in the people who called themselves His disciples, but in Him alone. Their belief drove them past social barriers, beyond walls of fear, through minefields of familial rejection, over mountains of pain, and into realization of the tangible substance of their belief. Some fought through painful physical limitations. Others battled the chains of confusion on the battlefields of their mind. Still others, controlled by powerful forces unseen and unfathomable to the human mind, grabbed onto the knot at the end of their rope. They held onto their belief that there is hope in believing because believing is seeing!

It is my hope that you will read these vignettes looking for ways in which you can identify with the characters in these stories. All of us either have been these people or know people like them. We may have never met Levi the tax collector, but each year April 15th gives each one of us an indication of the attitude people had toward him. Leprosy is almost nonexistent today in America, but every society has its lepers, such as the homeless or the AIDS patients. Many of the characters in the stories you will see were a lot like you and me. They are looking for hope in a hopeless world. They are looking for help in a helpless generation.

Each story has one thing in common. When confronted with a problem, each of these people finds the answer in one source. Each of these people is trying to fill in the gaps in his or her life, holes filled only when they see Him. When asked if there was anything worse than being blind, it is believed Helen Keller responded, "Yes, to have sight but no vision." It is my desire that you get a vision of this Jesus. Don't allow what you know from your past to blind you from the truth. I promise, if you will search for truth you will find it because truth is looking for you. I hope you will see Him because I know He is looking for you. Remember, believing is seeing. The seeker finds, the believer receives, and the receiver wins the prize of His hope.

After you have read the vignettes, I will return and we can reflect together on what you have seen. I will see you at the end.

Chapter One

Blind Too

Mark 10:46-52

IT had grown cloudier every day until…darkness. I wasn't always blind, but it had been years since I had last enjoyed the beauty of a flower, the golden hues of a spring sunrise over the Sea of Galilee, or the comforting glance of a loved one. I didn't really appreciate them when I had sight, but now in this world of darkness, I missed them just the same.

I had spent most of my life pursuing the wealth of Jericho. The hustle and bustle of the market had been my workplace. All was well until the clouds rolled in, blocking all light from the sun. I had been banished to the land of eternal night. No moon. No stars. No light. What could I do when my only means of support was lost? Only one option had been left to me.

I always laid my things in the same place so preparation the next day was easier—coat here, cane here, satchel over there, sandals at the foot of my pallet. It had to be so since all sight had now gone. I hardly noticed it in the beginning. Some days it felt like I was walking in a fog. Hazy one day, blurry the next until nothing. One day, I woke to the darkness that is now my existence. It was as if I could not open my eyes. I had to do something. No doctors could help. My friends that had been there when business was good slowly found other interests. I couldn't blame them. I was going to be a burden to anyone willing to help. But I never became a burden, for there was no one willing. If it was me, I probably wouldn't have helped either. There had been others in the city who were blind, and I had walked around them like so many now walked around me.

I had to do something to live. My old job was out of the question. Begging was the only thing available to me. There was no interview, no one waiting in line competing for the job, and no hope of advancement. I could get in on the bottom floor—that was all there was, bottom floor. A dead-end job, if I could call it that. I was at the mercy of unconcerned passersby.

Every day I made my way to the same spot on the main road outside the city: 542 steps—turn left at the corner, 798 steps—turn right onto Main and head south, 1988 steps to my place of business. I would kneel there on the side of the road, legs under me as if in a posture of prayer. Truthfully, I was praying, praying for mercy from anyone who would show me some. Mercy is a rare commodity, so rare that the sound of the coins dropping into my bowl would sometimes shock me. There was a steady stream of weighty purses passing by, heading for commerce in Jericho. If they didn't give, I did without. I had nothing to offer, and yet I was looking for payment. It was a humiliating existence.

The loss of my sight had finely tuned my other senses. I could feel the vibration as people tried to slip past me unnoticed, un-giving. I could tell you, within a few coins, how much was in the purses of the liars who would announce they had nothing to give.

Suddenly I heard something strange coming my way. *What is all this noise and activity,* I wondered. *Was it a shepherd bringing his flock to market? No, the footsteps were too heavy to be sheep, and now I can hear voices. Too many to be the shepherd and his helpers.* This was a large crowd coming, and I could hear cries for help. Usually I could follow a conversation at 50 paces, but in this case, there were too many clamoring voices to follow. Finally, my curiosity got the best of me and I asked someone, "Friend, what is all the noise about. What is going on?" Abruptly he retorted, "Jesus is coming. He is almost here. Leave me alone."

Jesus? I thought. *Coming down my road past my place?* I had heard of Jesus of Nazareth. He was the prophet, the teacher, the healer. The *healer!* And He was passing by that day. Probably close enough that I could finally get His attention. I had heard many tales of how He had given a lame man back his legs, raised the dead, and healed leprosy. I had even heard He once healed a blind man who had been blind from birth. My situation was nothing compared to these. *Maybe He will be able to help me. My miracle would be easy for someone like Him. All I have to do is get His attention. How can I find Him?*

The crowd was too large, pushy, and selfish to allow me through. I had to do something. All I could do was call out His name. "Jesus! Son of David, have mercy on me!" Those around tried to shut me up, but I only cried out louder. "Jesus, have mercy on me. I am a needy man with no one to help me."

As I was wondering if I had been successful in my pleading, I heard Jesus say, "Bring him to me." As someone helped me through the crowd, I began to wonder what He would do. Just then, I felt His breath in my face, and He said, "What would you like Me to do for you?"

That was a strange question. I couldn't imagine that He was unable to discern my state. Certainly He could see what I needed. What did I want Him to do for me? Maybe He was unable to heal me and I should ask for the next thing on my list. Problem was, I had no list. There was no hope of ever receiving anything, so why have a list? No hope until now! Hope rose inside of me like a natural spring. It brought life as it bubbled up from deep inside, and I said, "I want to see again." That was all I said. No begging, no crying, no promise of changed ways. *Why didn't I try to sell Him on the job? Maybe if I try something else it will ensure the right response.*

Before I could reword my request, Jesus answered me, "Receive your sight. Your faith has made you well."

Flash! A deluge of light overwhelmed me, sending me to my knees. Warmth from the Son began at my head and traveled through every vein and vessel in my body until it reached my feet. Endless night had given way to the dawn of a new day, a new life. Immediately, I could see as clearly as before. There before me stood the provision to my need. When I saw Him, His eyes poured love and compassion into mine. All I could do was worship. This was no mere man with a gift to heal. He was more than a prophet, more than a teacher. He was the answer to every question, a light to dispel darkness. He had not only given me sight; He had given me vision.

When the crowd saw what had happened, a party broke out. They all began to praise and worship Jesus. It was as if the air was filled with the sound of angels joining in as well. I was healed! I could see, really see! The flowers are more beautiful now. I spend time at the shore of the sea, waiting for the sunrise to paint its perfect mixture of gold and red across the azure sky. The look of the loved one is a cherished moment. Everything changed when I saw Him.

Points to Ponder

1. In what ways do you identify with the blind man's plight?

2. Have circumstances beyond your control ever irreversibly changed your life for the worse? How did you feel? What did you do to cope?

3. Have there been times when you walked away from someone in need, making excuses about why you couldn't help?

4. In what areas of your life might you suffer from blindness? How might Jesus want to bring you new vision?

Chapter Two

Jairus

Mark 5:22–43

*S*HE *has been sick for many days now and the doctors have left us with no hope. Day by day, she has grown weaker. Why has this happened to her? She was the picture of purity. Never has she caused problems, never disobedient, always willing to help. She was so loving and kind. She should be out playing with her friends, not lying in this bed dying. What can I do?* I asked myself as the feeling of helplessness overshadowed me. I had done everything a father of means would do. I had sent for all the best doctors, bought all the latest medicines, and yet I found no answer. What more could I do? I had been to the synagogue, but my friends, the other leaders there, only said, "We'll pray for her." Those words sounded so hollow now that I was the hearer instead of the speaker. There had to be an answer.

Where is an Elijah or Elisha, a miracle worker, when I need one? Someone to raise my daughter off of this sick bed? That's what I need. As that thought passed through my restless mind, I remembered, *Wait, there is an Elijah in the land. Several people thought that He was Elijah back from the grave. That Jesus guy from Nazareth, He has healed many. I've even seen Him do it. But what will my friends think if I go to Him? Many of them are already trying to find a way to get rid of Him. What if I go to Jesus and He doesn't heal her? He has seen me with those who are out to get Him. I can just see it now. I walk up to Him with my story, and He will recognize me as one of His accusers. This is the man who answers our questions even before we form the words in our mouths. He'll know me all right, and then He'll point out my hypocrisy in front of the crowd that is always following Him. I will be through in the synagogue for sure.*

As I thought about my status in the temple, the sounds of death from my little girl brought me out of my selfish concerns to the reality of the moment. *That is of little concern if I lose my little angel. My little flower is wilting before my eyes. She must have every chance to live no matter…no matter what it costs me.*

There was only one problem. How would I approach Jesus? *Uh, hmm, I know…"Master I know You have the ability to heal and that You certainly can see that we priests are all hypocrites and…" Oh that will never do. "Teacher, my little girl is so young and innocent and too young to die…"*

Frustration set in as my daughter's breathing became desperate. She seemed to be fighting for every breath. "We need to begin making arrangements with the mourners," someone tactlessly suggested.

At that, I ran out the door yelling, "I'm going to find Jesus!"

It mattered no more what would happen to me or my reputation. I knew Jesus was the only hope. "What will I say? How will I say it?" no longer plagued me. Getting to Jesus was all that mattered now, but I had to hurry. Death was quickly dragging my little girl away. I hoped I had not waited too long. *Why have I been so stubborn? Why didn't I go for Jesus sooner?* I asked myself. Then the answer rang through my mind, *Pride!* The one thing that will keep us in a lie when truth is beating down our door screaming "the house is on fire, get out or you will die." *Pride!*

There He was, in the middle of the crowd. *No time for pride here,* I thought. I ran, pushing my way through the mass of humanity. The dust from the streets, stirred by the multitude, mixed with the tears on my face. In desperation, I fell at Jesus' feet and begged Him, "Jesus, my little girl, only 12 years old, is sick and dying. Please come and heal her, please."

Jesus reached down, pulled me to my feet, and looked into my eyes. At that moment, when I saw Him, something seemed to say, "Don't be afraid." Jesus turned and began walking with me to my home.

But the crowd was pushing against us. They all wanted Jesus. *How could so many have such great need?* I wondered. Certainly none were as pressing as my little flower, who could die any moment. Pushing and struggling for every step toward my perishing little girl, I felt like I was in a bad dream. One of those dreams where I know where to go and how to get there, but can only move in slow motion. My mind is racing 90 miles a minute, but my body is in low gear, sometimes seeming to go backward rather than forward.

Then the last thing that needed to happen, happened. In the huge crowd, everyone pushing and shoving to touch Jesus, He stopped and asked, "Who touched Me?" Everyone began denying it, as if touching Him meant they had broken some unwritten law. Then Jesus clarified His question, saying, "Someone touched Me, and I felt healing power leave My body."

Just then a woman stepped forward and said she had touched Him. Then she went into some story about how she had been sick for so long, doctors couldn't help, da ta da ta da, yea, yea, yea. *She's healed; let's get going,* I thought. *My little girl is dying; this woman is healed. Let's go!*

As Jesus was addressing the woman, one of my friends arrived with the bad news. "Your daughter is dead. Don't bother the teacher any more." Pain shot through me like a million flaming arrows. Stunned by the announcement and the lack of compassion with which it was delivered, I almost fell to my knees. *Why had the crowd been in the way? Why did Jesus have to stop and talk to that woman? If He had come sooner, my little girl would be alive now. If only I had not been worried about what others thought and came sooner; things would have been different.*

As I was grieving and wrestling with the "whys" and the "if only's," Jesus once again looked at me and said, "Do not be afraid; only believe and she will be made well."

There was something about His eyes; when He said, "Don't be afraid," all my fear left and my strength returned. My step was confident as the healer and I walked to my house. We could hear the mourners long before we arrived at my home. But it seemed like the louder they got the stronger my faith grew.

When we arrived, Jesus started into the house, and when the mourners started to follow, He stopped them at the door. He allowed only me, my wife, and a few of His disciples to enter. Seeing her lifeless body and the hopelessness in my wife's eyes was almost more than I could bear. Tears began to flow freely. It was an indescribable moment of pain and despair to see my cherished little angel, who was always one who brought joy to our lives, laying there in the still look of death.

"Do not weep. She is not dead but sleeping," Jesus said.

Everyone in the room was shocked and even began ridiculing Jesus for making light of the situation. "The little girl is dead. Anyone can see that" several said.

Then Jesus made everyone leave the room. A few moments later, Jesus appeared at the door and said, "You need to prepare a meal; this little girl is hungry."

As she stepped through the door, I could hardly believe my eyes. My little flower, my angel, stood there as healthy and alive as before the sickness. A flood of emotion overwhelmed me like the spring floods of the Jordan. All propriety left my being. Jump, shout, cry, dance, cry, shout, cry—what a celebration, for my daughter, who was dead is alive again! All concern for what the religious leaders would think was gone. No thought of what if, why, or why not, entered my mind. Jesus had healed her; no, He had raised her from the dead; what a thought, what a reality.

"Do not be afraid, only believe," were the words He said on the road. I have to admit my faith was small. But it was enough when I brought it to Jesus. Everything changed when I saw Him.

Points to Ponder

1. Have you ever felt the sort of desperation that Jarius felt? Why? How did you respond?

2. Have you ever been impatient with other people's needs because your own seemed so pressing? What can you learn from Jarius's story that might change your perspective?

3. Are there areas of your life (your dreams, desires, emotions) that feel dead? Can you bring them to Jesus and ask for His resurrection power?

4. Do you or anyone you know need supernatural healing in your body? How can you push past your fears and questions to invite Jesus into your situation?

Chapter Three

Number Ten

Luke 17:11-19

W AKING from my normal, restless, and interrupted sleep, I began inspecting to see what
was and was not there—attached and still a
part of me. It seemed lately, every morning I literally woke
up beside myself—a new man or at least a different man
because I hadn't felt "new" in years. Now in the latter stages
of the disease, I often wondered how much longer I would
be around. *How much longer will my family have to deal with
the shame of my situation? If only someone—a thief or a mad-
man—would show me mercy and take my life,* I thought. But
even the most evil people ran when they saw me. Leprosy,
the greatest protection one could have. It seemed even the
wild beasts were repelled by it. Maybe the stench of death

told them "stay away"; who knows? All I knew was, it was another day, and I had to live through it somehow.

"Hey guys, what shall we do today? Dig through the dump or beg from afar?" It had become a sad joke to even ask the question because the dump had been our only source of existence for years. Since our leprosy had become so evident and hard to hide, even our closest friends and most of our families had stopped bringing food and supplies. Mainly they had stopped for fear of catching the disease. But the shame of having a friend or relative in this situation—well, let's just say it would have been better if we had died long ago. At least between the ten of us we usually found something worth eating.

"Might as well head for the dump; begging is useless. We can't even get close enough for them to hear us." We ten partners in pain set out for the dump outside the village. We had no way of knowing how our lives were about to change. It was a day like most other days until one of us looked up. He asked, "Isn't that the prophet everyone has been talking about? You know, the One who has made the priests so angry. The One who talks about God's coming Kingdom as if it were already here."

"What is His name?"

One of the ten said, "I think it's John the Baptist."

Still another said, "No, He is Elijah or Elisha come back from the dead."

Then I said, "No, His name is Jesus. He is the One who has raised the dead, a little girl I think, and gave sight to a man who had been blind since birth, and…" as the words were crossing my lips, we all had the same thought. Looking at each other with the same realization racing through our minds, no one spoke for what seemed to be hours. No one wanted to say it first, but we all knew we were thinking alike.

Finally, after what seemed an eternity, one of the others spoke up and said, "We probably couldn't get close enough for Him to touch us, if He even would."

Another said, "Yea, He would turn and run at the first sight of us approaching."

In the midst of their discussion, I cried out in desperation, "Jesus, Master, have mercy on us!" I had done it. Something inside me had cried out, knowing all I had to do was get to Jesus! What happened next seemed eventless.

Just as I had yelled at Him, Jesus yelled back, "Go and show yourselves to the priests." That was all. No dramatics. Not even a touch.

The others thought out loud, "Oh well, we tried." They were probably afraid. But as I turned and began walking, they followed. As we were walking, everyone began to gain strength, and what started as a slow, agonizing walk broke into an energetic run. The closer we got to the temple, the stronger we got. Then I looked down. The fingers I seemed to have misplaced were back on my hands. My skin was no longer the color of death, but life was now coursing through it like before. The snowy whiteness of the leprosy had been melted away by the *Son*.

I yelled, "Hey guys, praise God Almighty; I am healed." The others looked and realized that we had all been healed as we were walking. "We must return and thank Jesus for what He has done," I stated, but the others began talking about going through the cleansing process of the law or about a joyous return to their families. Someone even spoke about returning to the family business. All I could think about was returning to Jesus to thank Him. I left them. I had to see Jesus.

I turned and ran to see Him. On the way, doubts began to rise. *Would He even allow me to thank Him? I am a Samaritan. He certainly couldn't have seen that at the distance from which He had yelled at us. Or maybe He had and that was the reason He didn't come closer. It was the Samaritan rather than the leprosy that had repelled Him.* Even though the thoughts seemed to get stronger, discouragement would not be victorious. I was healed, and I was going to thank Him.

There He was walking down the road. I ran and fell at His feet on my face and began to worship and glorify God. "Thank You, Master. All Glory to God and praise to the Almighty for what You have done."

Almost as if He hadn't noticed my adoration, Jesus asked, "Weren't there ten who were cleansed? Where are they, where are the nine? Are none of them coming to glorify God except this foreigner?" That word *foreigner* rang in my ears. He knew I was a Samaritan, the scourge of the Jews, a dog to the Greeks. *What would He do? Would He take back my healing and curse me to die a leper? Many of the Jews would.* As the thoughts of Jesus' prejudice and retaliation coursed through my mind, the statement He spoke rang through the confusion.

"Get up; go on your way. Your faith has not only brought health, but today it has brought you salvation and eternal life."

Not only had He accepted my praise and thanks, from a Samaritan no less, but also He healed me and gave me salvation. The others received health, but missed eternal life. In returning, I received all I needed.

Points to Ponder

1. Think of a time when you've felt like an outcast. Did you ask Jesus for help? If so, what did He do for you?

2. Have you ever felt unworthy to receive a touch from Jesus? Why? What might the leper's experience teach you?

3. What did the leper need to do after Jesus spoke the healing word? How can you respond in faith to healing and blessing that Jesus wants to release in your life?

4. Are there times in your life when you received an answer to prayer, but forgot to thank and worship Jesus for His goodness? Take time to recall those blessings and sincerely thank Him for them now.

Chapter Four

Levi

Mark 2:14

I rolled out of bed that morning just like I had for years. The only thing on my mind was who I would see today and how much I would be able to collect above the taxing authorities' requirement. That was the only amount I was really concerned about. Yes, I had to pay Rome, but with the power of Rome behind me and the people's fear of her retaliation, collection came easy. Now the amount above the tax—that was when one had to become especially creative. That was what paid the bills, furnished the home, and threw the parties. Oh, the parties!

The Roman occupation had its hardships for some, but it had been a windfall for anyone willing to turn his back on his family and friends. *Not bad for a Jewish boy who was always told "you will never amount to much," I thought. So what if my own people despise me. Everyone knows it is lonely at the top. It is a small price to pay to live in the lap of luxury. Besides, I have more friends now than before. Everyone loves my parties with the finest wine, food, and women. I have no place to put everyone at most of the functions. Maybe I should remodel, enlarge to accommodate the growing entourage. Well, maybe I will get with the architect this Sabbath and begin plans, but for now I must hit the bricks and begin the bilking.*

It was a day like any other day, or so I thought. There was no way I could have known or sensed what this day would hold. When I arrived at my favorite corner to set up collections, I didn't realize what was taking place just down the street. In a house nearby, people were gathering to hear "the teacher."

I watched with piqued interest as the crowd began to grow beyond the house. Usually these folks were milling around the market buying and selling. That was why I had chosen this spot. Everyone had to pass me, and collections were steady. With the profits from trading in the market, taxes were easily collected, and usually cash was readily available, but not today. Hours went by and few passed my way except those hurriedly moving toward the house that had now spilled its mob out windows and doors into the street. Why they had kept coming was beyond me. *What were they hoping to see or hear that would be worth that? Never mind. Soon it would be over and all those purses would have to pass by the tax table.*

I leaned over to the guards assigned to me that day and said, "Get ready boys. The harvest is plentiful, and the laborers are few." *Where did I hear that? Maybe it is original with me,* I thought. *Oh well, it sounded good.*

Just then several men came carrying some cripple on a stretcher. *He is pitiful,* I thought. I had seen him begging before and had passed by many times. *Where are they taking him? Certainly they don't think they can get inside that over-crowded house.* What I saw next amazed me—and then it got my creative tax collector's juices flowing.

The men climbed on top of the roof and began tearing tiles off to make a large hole. *I know they do not have a permit for that construction, and I have no record of it. Wait till they get through. I'll slap them with a hefty fine on top of the permit fees. Then there will be the surveys and...* as I was tallying up the final bill, I saw something that turned my thoughts from the financial profits to insatiable curiosity.

The potential tax delinquents began lowering the cripple through the roof into the house below. *Why?* I wondered. *What could they possibly be thinking? What is the purpose in lowering this man into an already crowded house? Was it to hear a man talk about the newest get-rich-quick scheme? Maybe they were planning a rebellion against Rome, but what good would a cripple be?*

As these questions ran through my mind, the strangest thing happened. The cripple who had just been lowered into the house came running and jumping down the street shouting, "I'm healed! Praise God, I'm healed!" *This was the man who was carried in on a bed,* I thought. *Now he comes running down the street carrying his bed?*

"Jesus is a healer!" "Can you believe what we just saw?" "Where can you see such miracles in all of Israel?" were a few of the comments I heard as the crowd passed by.

After seeing what I saw and hearing the people's amazement, my focus changed from collections to questions. *What manner of man can raise a cripple from years on a sick bed? What kind of man could draw a crowd like this without blood, booze, or broads? Could what I've heard about this Jesus be true? Many say He is the Messiah. The Messiah, could it be a true prophesy, or was it a myth?*

As I considered these things, the hardness of my heart began to melt away. The boyhood years of Scripture study preparing for bar mitzvah came back to me. *Is what Isaiah said really true; was Jesus the One he was talking about?* If it was true and Jesus was the Messiah, I knew I was in trouble. I had walked away from the truth, from Him, for my own gain. I had sided with Rome. I had broken every command and then some. Even if it was true, I had gone too far. There could be no hope for one like me!

Maybe He is the One, but He will have nothing to do with me. Even if I wanted, I thought, *I could never get to Him. Besides, what would Jesus have to do with the likes of me? "Scum-of-the-earth traitor" is what my own people call me.* As I was thinking and questioning, Jesus emerged from the house with His entourage in tow.

Just then, Jesus stopped at my table. When I peered into the eyes of Jesus, when I saw Him, my world came to a stop. For some reason, the noise of the marketplace, which had now become a buzz of commercialism, fell silent on my ears; all I could perceive was Jesus. All I could hear were the words that would change my life for eternity. All I could feel was love pouring out of eyes pure and clear like a fresh, cool spring. All I could smell was the fragrance of hope, the aroma of Heaven that rose from the words spoken. All I could taste was the sweetness of honey from the Rock.

Jesus said, "Follow Me." That was all. Just two words, "Follow Me." Yet with those two words, all of my questions were answered. All of my doubts were dispelled. These words were more than words; they were life. With them came not only hope, but also the fulfillment of the hope in my heart that Jesus would accept me.

I didn't understand it all, but I knew when I looked into those eyes that it was right, that He was right. When I saw Him, there was nothing to do but stand up and follow. No questions of where we were going, what we would do when we got there, what I needed to take, or what I should do with my things entered my mind. I heard one thing: just follow. And I did. I stood up, leaving my table, taxes, prestige, and status. Something in His eyes told me all my questions would be answered and all my needs would be met. All I knew was, *Now is the time to follow.*

Points to Ponder

1. What shifted Levi's attention from self to Jesus? Has this shift happened in your life? If so, how did the shift happen in your life? Are there areas where you still need to turn your eyes toward Him?

2. What does this story tell us about the power of miracles? Have you ever seen the miraculous happen? How did it affect you? Others?

3. Do you have unanswered questions about life, about relating to Jesus? What can you learn from Levi's experience?

4. What might Jesus be asking you to leave behind so that you can follow Him more fully?

Chapter Five

Denied

John 18:25; 21:1-17

I can't believe I said it! "I don't know Him. I swear on my mother's grave, I don't know Him." I even cursed the woman for saying it, as if she truly had mistaken me for someone else. *How stupid can you get?* One of the men who recognized me was a cousin to Malchus, the man whose ear I had cut off in the garden. But I said, "I don't know Him!"

I don't know the One who called me and said He would teach me to catch men like I had caught fish for years? I don't know the One who said, "Come to Me" on the lake, and I walked to Him on the water? I don't know the One who had me catch a fish only to find inside the fish the money we needed to pay our taxes? I had told Him I was ready to die for Him, and then I denied I even knew Him. Jesus told me that I would do it, deny Him three times before the rooster crowed twice. I did what He had said; He was right.

There I was, watching them beat Him and spit on Him. Someone would say, "Prophesy! Who struck You?" Then they would laugh. That laughter was driving me crazy when Malchus' cousin spoke up and said, "I know for sure he is one of them. He cut my cousin's ear off." I turned to him and cursed him and swore I did not know Jesus of Nazareth. The words were hardly out of my mouth when I heard the rooster crow the second time.

I looked at Jesus, and He raised His head till His eyes met mine. When I saw Him, I remembered what He had said. When He told me I would deny Him, I wanted to speak up, as I usually did, and tell Him, "No way; I will walk with You even to death." But something had prevented me from saying a word. Now it was true. I had denied Him as a friend, but most of all, I had denied Him as my Lord.

There was something about the way He looked at me. It wasn't an "I told you so" look, but rather an "It's going to be fine" look. At that point, it didn't matter. I had denied the only One who had been a true friend to me, and I had denied Him three times.

At that realization, I broke; I turned and ran away weeping. Gut wrenching cries and tears like never before came from the deepest part of me. I had betrayed Him like Judas. My life was over. *What good could I be in His Kingdom? What Kingdom? Who was I kidding? It's over! They will kill Him, and then they will seek us out and kill us too. Maybe,* I thought, *it would be better to be dead than to live with the realization that I had denied the only One who ever really loved me.*

They took my Lord and beat Him beyond recognition. They paraded Him around like some trophy or spoil of war. One of the Roman soldiers took some Judean thorns and made a crown. Then they placed it on His head and began marching around Him, mocking Him as a king. Then beating the crown down on His head with rods, they made the thorns go into His head, breaking on His skull and puncturing through the skin. Blood was running down His bruised and swollen face. The only place bloodier was His back, which had been beaten and cut until the flesh hung like ribbons. He was a bloody mess.

The only time I had seen more blood was on the Day of Atonement, when the priests would sacrifice all the animals to cover the sins of the people. And I had allowed this to happen, or at least I had done nothing to prevent it. *What if I had not denied Him that night? What if in the garden I had armed the disciples. If only I had asked Simon the Zealot to bring some of his bloodthirsty friends in to help defend Jesus—things would be different. What if I had...?* I could "what if" forever and it would not change the fact that I had denied Him.

The next three days were kind of a blur. All I remember is going back to the place where we had the last supper with Jesus. When I got there, the others were hiding there also. Then it happened. A banging on the door! They were here to get us! Someone had betrayed us just like we had betrayed Him. But when we opened the door, Mary and a few other women were there, and their faces were glowing. They began excitedly, "He's alive! He's risen!" Mary even said she had seen Him.

I bolted out the door, and as I was running to the tomb, John passed me by and saw the stone rolled away from the opening. I ran into the grave and saw the grave clothes and the head cloth that had wrapped His body—lying where the body had been. As I left, I wondered what had happened. *Did someone steal His body, but if they did, why did they take the time to fold the grave clothes? Where were the guards? Why would someone want to steal His body anyway?* As these questions went through my head, I returned to the upper room.

While we were there, two people came in speaking about how Jesus had appeared to them on the road to Emmaus. They spoke of how their hearts burned when He spoke. I longed to feel that burning again, but I feared those days were over for me. Suddenly, Jesus was there! The doors and windows were locked for fear of the Jews, but Jesus came in somehow. He said, "Peace be with you."

Then He showed us His hands and side. The excitement of seeing Him and the joy of His resurrection began to rise inside of me, but the guilt of denying Him would not let me go. It was like chains on my soul. The gut-wrenching I had felt that night returned and intensified each time He looked my way or spoke. When He would look at me, I would turn my face away. I couldn't bear looking into the eyes of the one I had denied.

Later that week, after Jesus had shown Himself to Thomas, I decided I was tired of dealing with it all. I was going back to the only thing I knew, the only thing I could do after blowing my chance with Jesus. I went fishing. When I spoke up, several of the others said they would go as well. We fished all through the night and caught nothing. I didn't know if we were rusty after not fishing for three years or if even that skill had been taken from me also.

As the sun was rising over the Sea of Tiberius, we were pulling in our last nets when we heard a voice from the shore. "Children, do you have any food?" *Just great! A customer ready to buy fish, and we have nothing to offer. Probably a large buyer too. They were usually the first ones at the shore in the morning to buy the day's catch.* I hated telling Him we had nothing, but when I did, He said, "Cast the net on the right side of the boat and you will catch some."

Normally suggestions from shore after a long night of not catching a thing were not heeded, but whether it was the lack of confidence in our skill or the fatigue of the moment, we cast our nets on the right side of the boat. Immediately our nets were beyond capacity. Usually the nets would have given way under the pressure, but it seemed they were woven with cords that could not be broken. John leaned over in awe and said, "That's no fishmonger; that's Jesus!"

When I heard that, I grabbed my coat, dove into the water, and headed for shore. Sure enough, it was Jesus. He had prepared a fire to cook us breakfast. There on the coals were bread and fish, already prepared. Jesus said, "Bring in what you have caught and come eat."

After we had eaten, we were sitting around the fire talking when Jesus asked me, "Simon, do you love Me more than these?"

I answered, "You know I have a great affection for You, Lord." What a lame answer, but it was all I could say. I dared not be so boastful as before by pledging a love till death.

As I was evaluating my answer, Jesus replied, "Then feed My lambs." Then He turned again and asked, "Simon, do you love Me more than these?"

I answered, "Yes Lord, You know I love You."

He again said, "Feed My lambs." Then a third time he turned to me and asked, "Simon, do you have a great affection for Me?"

Three times He asked if I love Him. I denied Him three times. Did He have to rub salt in the wound? I finally answered, "Lord, You know all things. You know I have great affection for You."

With that He replied, "Feed My sheep."

As I was sitting there having my pity party, I began to realize that the three questions were not criticism. They were rather affirmation. Jesus was never one to put us down, but instead He would lift us up. He had not taken this opportunity to shame me in front of my peers, but instead to let me know the denial had not made me unworthy to serve Him. *Wow! He can use me! I love Him, I believe Him, I'll obey Him.*

It was at that moment I saw Him. Maybe for the first time I really saw Him! They were the same eyes that had looked through the blood of the beating, the eyes that now said, once again, follow Me and I will teach you to catch men just like you catch fish. That was when I saw Him!

Points to Ponder

1. Have you ever denied Christ because you were afraid of what others thought? How did you feel afterward?

2. When you feel like you have failed Christ, what do you do? What do you think Jesus wants you to do in those situations?

3. Peter returned to fishing. What sorts of things are you tempted to turn to when life gets hard, instead of running to Jesus?

4. What is the significance of Jesus asking Peter three times, "Do you love Me?" How did this redeem Peter's three denials? When have you experienced this kind of redemption of your failures from Jesus?

Chapter Six

The Blind

John 9

CROWDED streets were both a blessing and a curse. On the one hand, as a beggar, more people meant more potential money, but on the other hand, getting a good spot was more difficult with only a stick to guide me. Why did I always set up my begging near the temple? Was it the hope of catching some penitent worshiper looking for a way to ease his conscience or the hope that one day a prophet would show up, someone like Elijah or Elisha who had the power to heal? Maybe it was because old habits die hard, but whatever it was, I had decided if I didn't collect enough that day, I was finding another, more profitable spot.

Finally, after struggling through the unusually busy streets, I came to the spot that had been my only source for years. Some days were pretty good, those when I actually scraped enough together to have fresh bread instead of stale, hot soup rather than leftovers. That was the life I lived for so long that I felt almost no hope of change. There had always been stories of God healing people of their maladies, but never had I heard a story of someone blind from birth receiving his sight. All I had to hope in was begging as a way of life.

By the temple there was always a steady stream of religious types coming and going. You would think it would be a good place to get help, but too often the religious were the ones who would pass by without so much as a hello or God bless you, much less financial assistance. Then it happened. Like so many times before, I heard a voice say, "Teacher, whose sin caused this man to be born blind, his parent's or his?" *Oh great,* I thought, *another group of religious wannabes desiring a lecture on the evil in my life that had caused my plight.* I always thought that was the dumbest question. *How could my sin have caused me to be **born blind**? How could I have sinned in the womb?* The question angered me because I had heard it, or something like it, so many times before. Then usually some pompous preacher would pontificate as if he really had some understanding about me and my condition. But as yet, none of them had been able to convince *me* of their mental prowess.

I decided it was a good time to leave and find another spot rather than sit there and listen to another sermonette about how evil I or my parents had been. As I was struggling to get to my feet, I heard the teacher speak words that caused me to slump back into my place. "It is neither this man's sin nor his parent's that has caused him to be born blind."

I thought, *It's about time someone said it. I could not have sinned before I was born, and my parents were good people. Besides, what kind of a God would punish a child for the sins of his parents?* As I was thinking these things, what the teacher said next startled me back to the discussion. "He has been born blind so that the works of God, which have been hidden in Me, can be made known."

What did He say? I had been born blind so the works of God could be made known? I didn't understand what He was saying. *What works had been hidden in Him, and why did they have to be hidden? When were they going to be revealed? When they are revealed, what will they look like?* Questions kept coming as I sat there shocked by what the teacher had said.

All I knew was *hidden* seemed to be the operative word. Either these "works" were hidden in another, or they were hidden so deeply in this one that they were never to be revealed. That was usually what happened. The teachers would end their diatribes with something like, "These things are yet to be revealed," or "You will understand as you grow and mature," leaving the students with nothing more than they had before.

When I heard "hidden," I wanted to yell, "Ollie, Ollie, oxen free" to call those words from their hiding place, but before I could utter a word, the sound jerked me from my thoughts back to reality. I had heard that sound many times before. It was the recognizable sound of human saliva being expelled from someone's mouth. Usually the sound was followed by the unmistakable feeling of moisture in my face. But this person had at least been a bad shot, which was unusual for a group of students being trained by a good Rabbi. With my experiences as a reference, I thought Spitting 101 was the first course the students had to pass because so many had been able to hit me at a full gallop headed to temple.

Waiting for the next shot to be taken, I was shocked by the coolness of some substance being smeared onto my eyes. I wondered what it was, and then I realized it was the spit mixed with the dirt of the streets. I couldn't believe it. Whoever spit at me had missed so he had to humiliate me by smearing mud in my face, giving his cohorts a good laugh. But that didn't happen. No laughter came from this crowd. Maybe they were as shocked as I was that someone would be so unfeeling. But there was something about the way He rubbed the mud into my eyes. It was gentle. It reminded me of the times my mother had rubbed my eyes with a salve to relieve the discomfort of the dryness. Tenderness at such a time seemed out of place.

Then the teacher said, "Go wash in the pool of Siloam." I thought, *You bet I'll go and wash. You are lucky I can't see You to get a hold of You. I would teach You a thing or two, oh great teacher.* I was getting up to leave when I realized, again, that no one was laughing. That, along with the gentle medicinal touch, left me wondering what had really happened. I got to my feet and began to make my way to the water. As I was walking and thinking I realized that no one was following to humiliate me or point out my situation. It was as if I was moving unnoticed by any passersby. I reached the pool and started washing away my embarrassment. The first water touched my eyes and something began to happen. There was a burning unlike I had felt in years. It wasn't painful, but the burning seemed to be warming a place long since dead and cold.

Confused by it, I washed frantically. The burning that had been in my eyes only had now engulfed my whole being. It was warming me from head to toe. I hadn't ever felt life coursing through me like this. Then when the last of the mud was washed from my eyes, I opened them, readying myself to stumble back to my spot to beg some more. Expecting darkness, I was thrown to the ground by a flood of light. *What was that? I must be dreaming, but I thought I saw something.*

Gathering myself, but afraid to open my eyes, I struggled to my knees. Bent over the pool, I opened my eyes once more to see the face of a stranger. *Is this a vision in my head?* I wondered. I closed my eyes, and it went away. I opened my eyes, and there he was again. The stranger seemed to reappear every time I opened my eyes.

I reached to rub my eyes, and at the same time, the stranger reached for his eyes. I grabbed my nose. He grabbed his. I grabbed my beard. He grabbed his. As I spoke, he began to say the same words, but my voice was the only one

I heard, and I realized—I was seeing myself for the first time ever. "I can see!" Even as the words came out, chills shot through my body like an early morning mountain chill. "I can see. My hair, my nose, my beard, that's no stranger; that's me! I can see me!"

The joy and excitement pulled me to my feet so fast it made me dizzy. This was a new experience. Walking with sight left me a little disoriented, but I would learn. All I knew was I had to find the teacher of that group of students. He had healed me, and I had to know who He was. I ran through my old neighborhood, and many who knew me said, "Isn't that the beggar who always begs by the temple?"

Someone else said, "I always knew he was faking it."

Still another answered, "I knew him as a child. He was not faking. He was as blind as a bat, but something has happened."

None of it deterred me. *No need to explain now. There will be plenty of time later. I have to see the teacher. See the teacher—* the thought brought floods of tears and joy. Being able to see the One who had given me what was never mine, had been unimaginable just moments before. This teacher had been able to do in a moment what no other had been able to do in my lifetime.

Finally someone stopped me and asked, "How were your eyes opened?"

I told him that a man, a teacher near the temple, whom I thought someone called Jesus, placed clay in my eyes and told me to go and wash in the pool of Siloam. I went, washed, and now could see! I saw several people break for the pool, and then someone asked where could they find this Jesus? I told them I was looking for Him also. I didn't know where He was, but I was going to find Him.

Just then one of the temple guards grabbed me and took me before the high priest and the Sanhedrin. I wondered why the guards had brought me to see them. *"See them," who cares why?* I thought. *I get to* "see them"! The thought made me as giddy as a new bride marrying her true love. I felt silly, but I could not stop laughing inside, and it finally came out.

The high priest asked, "How did you receive your sight?" It wasn't the question, but rather the tone in which it was asked, that brought me back to the sober surroundings of the court. But only for a moment.

When I began to tell them the story of what had happened, the spit, the clay, and the pool—the giddiness returned. "He made clay, rubbed it on my eyes, I washed, I see!" was all I could get out between laughs.

Then the debate began, "This man can't be from God. He doesn't keep the Sabbath laws."

Another said, "How can a man do such things as this, give sight to a man blind from birth, and not be from God? No one has even heard of such a thing in all of our history."

Then the debate turned to war. When there was a lull in the action, they turned to me and asked, "What do you say about this man who gave you sight? How did He open your eyes?" It was the same question they had already asked time and time again. I wondered, *Why is it when people do not get the answer they want they keep asking the same question?*

They then dragged my parents into the court and asked them to verify that I had truly been born blind. When they didn't hear what they wanted, the discussion returned to Jesus and what kind of man He was, His educational background, and where He was from.

Finally something inside of me rose up, and I said, "Why is it such a big deal where this man Jesus is from? He has given me my sight, something none of you could do, and we know that God does not listen to sinners, but if anyone is a worshiper of God and does His will, He hears them. Never before in all of history have the eyes of someone born blind at birth been opened. Why can't you accept this miracle you see right before you? You are blinder than I ever was. If this man is not from God, He could not have done this."

At that they turned on me and accused me of being one of His disciples. *I'm not yet,* I thought, *but as soon as I can find Him, I will be.* Then they accused me of being "completely born in sin," as if they weren't, and said I was ignorant and should stop trying to teach them. Then they threw me out—literally.

Finally I could continue my search for Jesus. As I was picking myself up from the dusty street, He touched my shoulder. He had been seeking me! Jesus, the One who had given me sight, was looking for me. Jesus asked me, "Do you believe in the Son of God?"

I told Him I'd believe in the Son of God if He would show me where He is. Then I looked at Jesus and He said, "You have seen Him." I began to look around for the One He was talking about when He finished, "I am He." When Jesus said that, I looked at Him as if I was seeing Him for the first time. This time, when I saw Him, I really *saw* Him for who He was.

I fell to the ground before Jesus and said, "I believe, Lord!" and I began to worship Him. I have worshiped Him ever since that day. He gave me physical sight that day, but I was able to really see when I *saw* Him!

Points to Ponder

1. Have others ever theorized about why you have experienced difficulties? How did it make you feel? What might Jesus say about your situation?

2. What did the blind man need to do to receive his healing? Was he even seeking healing? What does this teach you about Jesus?

3. Consider the contrast between the blind man's reaction to his healing and that of the religious leaders. How have you tended to respond to the miraculous? Why?

4. Are there areas in your life where you have stopped hoping for change? Ask Jesus what He has to say about those places of pain. How can you respond to Him with a heart of faith?

Chapter Seven

A Good Soldier
Matthew 27:54

I spent most of my career in Caesar's Praetorian Guard. I had seen enough deceit and manipulation to make me sick. Politics and power are two of the most corrupting forces in the world. I had seen the rise and fall of more than one Caesar and even the betrayal and execution of one by his closest friend. I had seen enough. I asked for a transfer to an occupying force somewhere, anywhere, just away from Rome and its cesspool of society. Jerusalem had seemed like a blessing from the gods. Maybe they were finally smiling on me after all I had been through.

Things were pretty tame in Israel. The Jews had no organized army. There were always skirmishes with the zealots, but that just kept the mind and body sharp. I loved the climate, and there was always plenty to do on my days off. All I wanted was to spend the rest of my time until retirement standing guard or escorting some dignitary. Retirement and collecting my pension were all I had on my mind.

We were coming up on the holiday season for the Jews, and that meant more time off. Things usually got pretty quiet since even the rabble-rousing zealots observed the holy days and caused little to no problems. That was the way it had been for the last three years. Quiet peaceful holidays, but this year was going to be unbelievably different.

A man named Jesus had shown up in Jerusalem about three years ago. I had just been transferred and was looking for simpler times. The first time I heard of Jesus was in the mess hall. Some of the other soldiers were talking about how He had made the religious leaders so mad they could spit. Evidently Jesus was talking about their laws and prophets without any special training. What was worse, the people were beginning to listen to Him instead of the recognized teachers in the synagogue.

Jesus came and went during those three years, and every time He showed up in Jerusalem, there was a stir. There were always crowds to control, but usually everything was peaceful. There was something different about this Jesus guy. He was always talking about love. He even said that we should love our enemies. That was a hard one for me to swallow because the only enemies I had were always coming at me with a sword ready to kill me. It was kill or be killed. That is hardly the time to spread love and cheer.

The closest I ever got to Him was one day while He was teaching. Many times Jesus would teach as He walked down the streets. That day, He walked right up to me and used me as an example of what He was teaching. I don't know all of what He was saying, but He pointed at me and said, "If someone asks you to carry his load for a mile, you carry it two. And if someone asks for your coat, give him your shirt also." I guess He used me because He had heard of the Roman law that stated we had the right to demand that a Jew carry our belongings for us, and they could not refuse. But what Jesus said went beyond the law.

There were many times when I saw and heard Him. Once I was almost persuaded to follow Him myself, but that would never do. *Maybe after retirement and the pension were secure, but I can't risk losing my security for old age.*

Another time I heard Him say He was the Son of God. This sent the Pharisees into a tizzy. They came to Pilate, my boss, and complained that Jesus was not only a threat to their religion, but that He was also undermining Caesar's authority. It wasn't long after that incident that Jesus was arrested and brought before Pilate. I don't know how they did it because the Temple Guards had tried several times before to capture Him to no avail. We called them the Temple Goofs, wannabes who were untrained and undisciplined compared to Rome's elite centurions.

This time was different because one of Jesus' disciples led the Temple Guards to Him. They pulled it off, and Jesus was standing before Pilate for judgment. After all his questions, Pilate was convinced there was no fault in Jesus. Pilate wanted to release Him. Even his wife urged him to do it, but in the end the people cried out for His death, and He was sent to me for crucifixion.

It was a horrible way to die for anyone, much less this man. He had done nothing wrong except get on the bad side of the religious nut in charge. *Politics, religion, and power all corrupt.* I wondered how this was different than Rome. But I had to see it through. It was my job, and I was a good soldier.

The scourging post was where most of them died. The beating was the most brutal thing that could be done to a human body. After the whip, called a cat of nine tails, was through with you, your flesh would hang from your weakened body in bloody strips like the wind-torn fabric of a scarlet flag. The whole time Jesus was being beaten, He said nothing. Not even cries for mercy were heard. When it was over, He was made to walk up the hill carrying His own cross. I wondered with amazement, *Where did He get the strength?*

I was in charge of this affair, and I had to make sure everything was done by the book. I had to watch every detail, so when they were ready to nail His feet and hands to the cross, I was standing over watching. Usually people would fight with whatever strength they had left, but Jesus laid down on His own and opened His hands to receive the spikes. It was as if He did it of His own free will. The pain had to be excruciating, but again, He said nothing.

I don't remember all He said while He hung between Heaven and Earth, but the two things I did hear, I will remember forever. I was standing guard to keep people at a safe distance. I looked up to see what was going on when His eyes caught mine. For the first time, I saw His eyes. They were penetrating to my core. What I usually saw from a cross was hate, but these eyes were comforting to me. Then what He said sent me spinning, searching for understanding. He said, "Father, forgive them. They do not understand what they are doing."

Was He praying for a god to forgive me? Praying for me in His dying state? At that point, everything I had lived for and believed became a blur. It is hard for me to tell you how, but something in His eyes told me He was the only truth there was.

Everything went out of focus. I don't know how much time passed, but I was awakened from my blurring stupor by what I came to realize were His last words, "It is finished. Father, into Your hands I commit My spirit." No sooner were the words spoken than there was an earthquake. The skies turned as black as midnight. This was no normal storm.

I spoke up and said, "This truly was a righteous man." But something had happened beyond the death of a man. It had to be true. He had to be who He said He was—the Son of God! *I just killed the Son of God, or did I? I don't know what to think. At least, before He died, He prayed for my forgiveness.*

After we took His body down from the cross, we gave it to one of His disciples. I was ordered to station a squad of soldiers to guard the tomb. The Pharisees were afraid His disciples would steal the body and proclaim He had risen from the dead. I posted the guards and went home for what I hoped would be a restful weekend. This had been the most stressful work week since I had arrived in Jerusalem.

The whole time at home, I could think of nothing but Jesus and how He had looked at me. No rest and no relaxation made returning to the job on Monday a pleasure. When I arrived at my post, the tomb guards were pulled into a meeting. I came in just in time to hear Pilate say, "Well then how do you explain it?"

The sergeant of my guards answered, "Sir, I know this is going to sound odd, but an angel appeared in an explosion of light and rolled away the stone. Then we all passed out on the ground. When we woke up, the angel and the body were gone."

They tried to explain it away, but I knew what had happened. I don't know how I knew, but I knew. He had risen just as He had said. His disciples had not stolen His body, as the Pharisees finally paid my guards to say. Those disciples were afraid of their own shadows. They would have never tried to go up against a squad of Roman soldiers. Nor would any of my soldiers have made up a story to cover up sleeping on the job.

Now I knew what His eyes were saying. They were saying, "I am in control of this. Believe in Me, and you can be forgiven." He had said something like that to one of the two men who were crucified with Him. Jesus had looked at him and said, "Today you will be with Me in paradise." I thought, at the time, that He meant they were both going to die that day. Now I realize what He meant was, "We are about to begin living, really living!" That was when I saw Him. For the first time I saw Him for who He was, Jesus the Savior.

Points to Ponder

1. The centurion was struck by Jesus' peacefulness and gentleness, even in the middle of great suffering. In what ways can you live with greater peace and gentleness in the midst of life's storms?

2. Initially the centurion chose not to follow Jesus because he didn't want to lose his secure retirement. In what ways have you chosen security and safety over a wholehearted pursuit of Jesus?

3. How did you feel reading the up-close description of Jesus being beaten and nailed to the cross? What of it brought new understanding to you about the suffering that Jesus experienced? How did it impact your heart?

4. Why did the centurion respond differently to the empty tomb than the religious leaders? What impact did Jesus' prayer for forgiveness have on his heart? How do you respond when you are confronted with your sinfulness?

Chapter Eight

Physically Challenged
Mark 2:1-12

THE pain was so bad that all I could do was lay there. My joints had long ago seized and locked like a steel trap exposed to the salty air of the Dead Sea. The crippling disease seemed to creep upon me slowly, but not as slow as my days had become. The immobility had turned the seconds of the clock to hours. It seemed like the sand in the hourglass fell in slow motion, one grain at a time. I would have ended my life if I had been able to move.

Instead my life amounted to lying on my bed on some street begging for alms to buy food to keep myself from starvation. My family and friends had long since deserted me, unable to care for my day-to-day needs. There was a time when strangers would buy me a meal or help in some way, but lately it had seemed that even they were repulsed by the filth I had become. Being unable to bathe or even clean up after myself had left me a mess.

Who could I have been? What could I have accomplished? If only I had not been crippled... The questions ran through my head often, even though I realized there was no answer. My dwindling hope, my desire to be well, was even eroding. With no hope and little desire, desperation was beginning to set in. I faced yet another long, unfruitful day of lying in complete public humiliation, crying out for help that so seldom came. *Maybe today I will just lay silent and do the only thing I can to take control—starve.*

In the midst of this pity party, I felt the bed I was laying on lifting from the street. "What is going on?" I asked the four men who were now carrying me down the street. When no answer came, I began to question myself. *Will they kill me? Maybe they will end this miserable existence that is my life. But they aren't headed out of the city, but rather toward the center. Why? Are they going to make a spectacle of me first and then end it all? It doesn't matter anymore; soon it has to be over.* The thought seemed to reverberate in my mind as a positive thing.

We headed right past Levi's tax table. He was always careful to make sure to collect the tax on what little I was able to beg for. Then as we passed Levi's collection booth, I heard the crowd. *They have gathered a large number of people for my humiliation,* I thought. *Maybe they are going to stone me. That means it will be over sooner—more stoners, less time. Not the way I would choose to die, but then again, I have no choice in how I live.* The only thought I had was that anything was better than one more day in this diseased state that I had been banished to.

As we passed through the crowd, they hardly even noticed me. Neither my appearance nor aroma turned a head or nose. They were all focused on something that took all of their attention. Then one of the men carrying me said, "We will never get him in there."

Another answered him and said, "You're right; let's drop him through the roof."

The third one said, "I'll get a rope."

So that was how they were going to do it, hang me. Oh well, that would be faster than starving. Drop, pop, and it would be over. Then, as I was thinking about the end, they began to pull the roof tiles off of the house. I said to them, "Wouldn't it be easier to find a tree to do the job?"

One of the men looked at me with a puzzled smile and said, "Relax, it will be over soon."

Man, can you believe it? I thought to myself. *He is smiling. He is enjoying this just a little too much.* Thinking they would place the rope around my neck, I was surprised when they tied it to the four corners of my bed and began to lower me through the hole they had just made in the roof. Slowly and gently they lowered me down into a house that was so full of humanity they seemed to burst out the doors and windows and spill into the streets. I kept waiting for them to drop me to my death, but instead I felt the bed come to rest gently on the floor beneath. When I opened my eyes, I saw peering through the hole in the roof four faces smiling like children on their birthdays looking at the gifts meant for them, wondering what was in the beautifully wrapped packages. *What are they seeing? It is certainly not my emaciated, filthy form.*

Then I saw Him—the preacher from Nazareth. *Certainly He wasn't part of their death plan. Why have they brought me here?* I wondered. Then my eyes met His. Jesus looked at me, and something changed. The peace from His eyes said, "Do not be afraid." He looked at me and said, "Man, your sins are forgiven."

I was reeling from the statement, trying to figure it all out, when Jesus looked at the scribes and Pharisees who were there and answered their unspoken questions. How He knew what their questions were, I did not know, but it had to be the right one because of the response He got from them. Jesus spoke, "Which is easier, 'Your sins are forgiven' or 'Get up and walk?' But so you will know that I have the power to forgive sin…" He turned to me and said, "Get up, pick up your bed, and go home."

As He was saying those words, I felt like oil was being poured all over me; then it was like fire inside me. Strength came back to the muscles that had long ago atrophied, and my joints began to pop and crack loose. I jumped to my feet almost as if powered by a force outside of my own. Joy flooded me so that I began to dance and shout. God had touched me. I ran through the crowd telling everyone that I was healed—jumping, shouting, and dancing down the streets. What had been my place of affliction was now my place of great joy. What I had so long been under suddenly became under my feet when I saw Him.

As I look back, I realize it wasn't my faith that healed me. Jesus touched me because of those men who carried me to Him. That was the reason for their smiles. They knew what was about to happen. I didn't have the strength or the hope to go myself, but they carried me to Jesus. Because of their faith, I found new life.

Points to Ponder

1. Have you ever felt paralyzed in an area of your life? Why? Were you able to find freedom? How?

2. The paralytic's life was so bad that he wished for death. Have you ever felt suicidal? What does Jesus offer in the midst of such hopelessness?

3. What does Jesus' question to the Pharisees mean? How does it apply to your life?

4. Have you ever been so overwhelmed by life that you couldn't get the help you needed until some friends came along and "carried you to Jesus"? What did such an experience teach you about the Body of Christ?

Chapter Nine

Wild Thing

Matthew 8:28-34

A S the sun rose over the lake, I began being warmed in its rays. I had made it through another torturous night. In my sane moments, questions plagued me. *What is wrong? What makes me act like a mad man one moment and then like myself the next? Why do I tear at my clothes and live naked in a graveyard?* Even my family had long since written me off as crazy and not worth the time because I was "dangerous."

What are these voices I hear? How am I able to break the chains they put on me? Why do I wake up naked and bleeding, lying in a graveyard, not knowing where I have been or what I have done? It reminded me of times, before the craziness set in, when I used to attend wild parties and drink until I passed out. That was long ago. I had reached the point where I couldn't even buy food and lodging much less wine.

"No! No! You can't do this! Leave me alone. Go away, I, I, I don't want you…" I shouted, struggling to maintain control.

An evil voice laughingly screamed inside my head, "You don't want? You have no choice in the matter. You are ours to do with as we wish."

Just as before, all I could do was run screaming, trying to get away from them. They laughed at my futile attempts to flee from them—the beings who had taken up squatter's rights in me. Truthfully, I had invited them in by living a life conducive to them. The place had been prepared for them by years of raucous living and a total disregard for right and wrong. I had abandoned righteous living for what felt good and was immediately available. The black and white of wrong and right had grayed into "if it feels good, do it" and then into "if it feels this good, I don't care if it is wrong."

Now I would give all the instantaneous pleasure up for one moment of peace. *Peace, what is that like?* I couldn't remember because every time my mind would wander down the path toward peace, *they* would tear at me, run me into a briar, make me cut myself with a stone, or whatever it took to black out any thought of hope or faith. The darkness would come in the middle of the day. Even though the sun baked my exposed flesh, the chill of the night was so real in my mind that it would cause me to shake.

"Miserable existence." "Why should he be allowed to live?" "It would be an act of mercy to stone him." These were a few of the comments I heard from passersby when and if they ever passed by. It had been a long time since that had happened. Even those who would have ended my life were afraid to come anywhere near me. They feared for their lives.

One day, as the wind blew off the lake, I found myself lying on the shore wet, partly from the waves lapping at my feet and partly from my own sweat and blood as a result of another night with my "friends." It had been an especially treacherous, torturous night. The "friends" had done everything they could to end my life. Part of me wished they had succeeded, but something inside me seemed to fight as if there was a hope of victory.

Victory? I questioned, *How can I win in this battle against so many?* In the beginning it hadn't been so difficult; in fact, it had been pretty manageable. It seemed like the only time the first "friend" showed up was at the parties. But that wasn't a problem because everyone loves a party. Besides, he was always gone the next morning, or so I thought. I decided to go to that psychic advisor, and it seemed I picked up a few of his friends, and they moved in.

After that, everywhere I went, my "friend" kept inviting more and more "friends" in until it got so crowded in there that I lost control. They were in charge, and there was nothing I could do. *Why did I fight so last night?* I questioned. *Why didn't I just let them win?* All night it had seemed like they had me on the ropes, ready to deal the fatal blow, and then they would stop. There I was in a pool of my own blood, beaten and cut up by my own hands, in excruciating pain and misery. *Why wouldn't they finish me off?* Something told me that was not the way they did it.

Pulling myself to my feet to walk back to the graveyard to find some place to lay and rest, I heard something on the lake. As I turned to see what or who it was, my "friends" returned with a vengeance and threw me to the ground as if to hide me from what was on the water. I struggled against them to see what had brought them back to torment me again.

I heard His voice before I saw Him. "Come out of him."

The sound of that voice caused my "friends" to tear at me as if they were the ones in pain. The pain and torment was worse than ever before. Just then, they spoke through me to this man, "What have I to do with You, Jesus, Son of the Most High God? I beg You, do not torment me!"

Jesus asked, "What is your name?"

As I started to answer, they took control of my voice again and said, "Legion, for there are many of us here." Then they begged Jesus not to send them into the abyss, but to send them into some pigs on the hillside. And Jesus did.

I felt immediate peace! Relief came so suddenly that I felt as though it had all been a dream. A clear thought, the first in years, filled my mind. Then I saw Him, the One who had spoken the words that had freed me. When I saw Him, everything else blurred into the moment of complete peace pouring from His eyes—the eyes of my deliverer.

I didn't understand all that had just happened, but I knew I wanted to follow this One who had set me free. No one else had even stopped to try and help, yet a moment in the presence of Jesus and I was free indeed! I had not even asked Jesus for help. Jesus, the Savior, the Deliverer, saw my need and met it.

"Please, Lord, let me come with You. I want to know You more. I beg You, don't send me away. I will be Your slave, carry Your bags, cook Your meals—anything. Just let me go with You," I said.

Jesus told me to go home and tell everyone what had happened. I went through the town, among the people who had seen me bound by demons, and proclaimed the freedom that I had found in Him, Jesus. I did it, and they ran Him out of town. They had been afraid of me, but now that I was sane, they were afraid of the one who had the power to set me free. That sounded like insanity to me. I see now why He wanted me to stay. Jesus and I have a lot of work to do.

Points to Ponder

1. Have you or anyone you know had experiences with demonic possession or influence? How did it compare to what the demoniac in the story experienced?

2. How do you (or would you) feel when you encounter people who are demon possessed? Do you want to help, or do you avoid them? Why?

3. What in the demoniac's life opened the door for his "friends" to come in? Are there things in your life that could be an open door to hindrance or control by demons?

4. What can you learn from the demoniac's experience in returning to his home and sharing his testimony? Why do you think the people were not excited to meet Jesus too?

Chapter Ten

Just Another Criminal

Luke 23:39-43

TODAY is the day! Unbelievable! Finally caught, tried, convicted! It's true that I am guilty of what they say, but do I have to die? It is such a horrible death—the cross. I should have fought the guards when they captured me. Maybe one of them would have ended my life at that moment, I thought. But like most of my life, the answer had come too late. Impulse had driven me to this place, and no amount of creative thinking would get me out of this mess that a life of criminal activity had produced. I probably deserved the treatment I was receiving, but it was still hard to be in the predicament and not wonder what it would have been like if only I had been raised in a different neighborhood, with different parents, a higher financial status. *If only, if only...who am I kidding? More than one of my childhood friends has risen above the life we were born into. Why didn't I?*

Choices. Choices made in an instant that led to more ill advised decisions. Soon the force of my past decisions was ushering me around with no ability to regain control. That was the way it was. At first I had the control; then I chose the easy way. It appeared to be slow and easy-going—a wide road with a lot of leeway. I could go far to the right and play all the way back past center to the left side and then back again.

As I traveled the road, it got more narrow and steep, but my lifestyle was still in the weaving mode. Pretty soon I ended up off the road, headed down the mountainside with no control, building up more and more speed until I crashed into the bottom, lower than I was when I started. When I was able, I would get up and try, without success, to dust off the results of my crash. Then I would turn and start up the same road, thinking this time I would beat it. *I know where the pitfalls are. I know where the road gets narrow and rough, and I will make it to the top this time.* Why this time? I had not been able to do it any of the many times before. But I would go again anyway because it was the only way I knew. There had to be a better way!

Here they come. What could they want now? "The Post for you scum!" the guard barked. I had seen the results of the beating, but could only imagine the pain. *Such a beautiful room for such a horrible duty,* I thought. The whole room was made of solid marble so after the deeds were done they could come in with barrels of water and wash out the day's duty into the drains at the lower end of the scourging hall.

I must have been the first that day for the floor, usually covered with the blood and bits of flesh from previous victims, was fresh and clean. As they tied me to the post in the center of the marble room, the coolness of the floor comforted my feet. Then short-lived comfort gave way to excruciating pain as the whip tore away my flesh, exposing bones and muscle. I know now why many do not live past the Post. Thirty-nine lashes seemed to take forever. Every inch of my body was beaten, bruised, and bleeding. *Could death not be merciful? Must I live through this only to be hung on a cross? Haven't I paid for my sin enough? Could this be the last breaaaaathhhhh…*

"Wake up!" screamed the guard as he kicked me to my knees. Dazed by the loss of blood and the kick to my ribs, I barely felt the ropes on my arms as they tied me to the wooden beam I was to carry up to the hill. I had lived through the beating and was going to die on a cross. Shoved out into the street with two other unfortunate, yet undoubtedly deserving souls, we began the trek up to the place of the skull. The one in the front was one of my cohorts. We had been involved together in many jobs before, but this was to be our final hurrah. What a way to end!

The man behind me was familiar, but I could not place Him. I had never worked with Him before but His face was one I didn't forget. Where had I seen Him before? *Maybe in jail…no I would remember that. Who is this guy?* He had been beaten worse than I had, and the guards had played their games with this man. His beard had been ripped from His face, and they had placed thorns on His head in the shape of a crown. They kept taunting Him saying, "If You are who You say You are, raise Yourself out of this situation." *What a joke. Who could possibly pull themselves out of this hell? Why someone would have to be as powerful as G…. That's it. I remember now. That man is Jesus.*

It was no wonder I hadn't recognized Him. He was covered in blood and beaten beyond recognition. *Why is He being crucified?* I wondered. *He had never done anything wrong.* I had seen Him do miracles in the streets of Jerusalem. Only two days before, I had seen Him ride into the city on a donkey. Where were all the people who had lined the streets that day to welcome Him? It seemed the same people were now screaming for His crucifixion. I had heard stories of many of the things He had done. They were good things—not worthy of this death. *He has great power. Why doesn't He use it now? Certainly someone who could raise the dead could overcome the soldiers. Maybe He could not do away with them, but He could at least get away.*

My thoughts had carried me to the hill. The end was near. As I hung on the cross, the strain on my arms and shoulders was only relieved by pushing up on the nail in my feet. The pain was excruciating, but I could not take my mind or eyes off of Jesus. The crowd and soldiers were making fun of Him. "Why don't You save Yourself?" they cried. "He has saved others, but Himself He cannot save." "If You are who You say You are, come down off the cross," shouted the onlookers.

Then He turned his head toward the sky and said, "Father forgive them; they don't know what they're doing." Hearing that, my thoughts went wild. *He is praying for those who are cursing Him! What kind of man is this? What kind of man? He is no man. He is the Son of God!*

Even the third man hanging alongside cursed him: "Some Messiah You are! Save Yourself! Save us!"

I had endured all I could. Something within me rose up, and I shouted to him, "Have you no fear of God? You're getting the same as Him. We deserve this, but not Him. He did nothing to deserve this." Then I said, "Jesus, remember me when You enter Your Kingdom."

When He turned His head, His eyes met mine. When I saw Him, He said, "Don't worry, I will. Today you will join Me in paradise."

After that, it was mostly a blur. Jesus cried out one last time, "Father, into Your hands I place My life!" Then He breathed His last breath.

Shortly after, I closed my eyes for the last time on this earth. When I opened them, I saw Jesus with His arms opened wide, welcoming me into His Kingdom. I had been changed, and it had happened when I *saw* Him!

Points to Ponder

1. Even in the midst of such great pain, the thief could not take his eyes off of Jesus. Have you ever experienced a situation where seeing Jesus distracted you from your pain and helped you find healing? What happened?

2. The thief also stood up for Jesus when everyone else was mocking Him. What do you think enabled him to do that when even Peter would not?

3. What happened in his heart when the thief stopped focusing on himself and started focusing on Jesus? How might that apply to your life?

4. What can we learn from the thief's "death bed" salvation? What might be significant about the fact that the first person saved through the new covenant of Jesus' blood was someone who never followed Jesus or did anything for Him in his life?

Chapter Eleven

The Seeker

Luke 19:1-10

I had heard of Jesus while collecting taxes in Jericho, but I had never seen Him. I had also heard all of the rumors and stories of how He could give sight to the blind, give new legs to the lame, and even raise the dead. *Probably just rumors,* I thought. *Things always get blown out of proportion. You should hear some of the rumors about me.* I have to admit that I was intrigued by the stories about Jesus, but not enough to pull me away from business. Business was great! Jericho was the best place in the Roman occupation to be a tax collector—import taxes, export taxes, sales taxes, income taxes, taxes, taxes, taxes. When I thought about it, I used to get light headed and begin to pant like a dog.

Up early one morning, I began to gather my thoughts and prepare for the day. I was always up before the servants to get the profits flowing. Prior to collecting, I had to tend to my other businesses in which I had partnered with the good folks of Jericho. *Partnered* was a loose term I used to describe the businesses that had gotten behind on their tax bills. When that happened, I was immediately invested. That was one of the benefits of the job. It seemed opportunity knocked at my door daily.

Even though business was good, I kept thinking there had to be more to this life. I had everything I could want—a big home, servants, money, prestige, and power; yet with all that, I felt empty. I was a chief tax collector with many collectors under my authority, but nothing filled the void in my soul. No matter how much I had, I always came up short.

Short, I hate that word. I've always been short. Before I was a tax collector, I was short of money. Now with plenty of money, I was short of respect, real respect. The only respect I got was when I came around to collect and people showed me respect to minimize the cost. *Short people get no respect! Oh well, enough of that. There is no profit in feeling sorry for myself. I'll just take my frustration out on those I see today. I have to get to work now.*

As I opened my front door, I saw a crowd in the streets. It was hard to leave the house because of the mass of humanity gathering. *Why are there so many people out so early? What could so many possibly be doing?* Pushing through the crowd that usually parted for me, I heard people talking, "He's coming. Yes, He should be here soon. Do you think we will see any miracles today?'

Who's coming? I wondered. *Had I missed a holiday, or could Caesar be visiting? Certainly he or someone of his status could draw a crowd of this magnitude. Whoever it is, he has to be very important,* I thought. *Why didn't my communications people tell me of this event? I'll have to have a talk with them when this is over. Heads will roll, but for now I have to position myself in the right place to be seen.*

Trying to push my way to the front of the crowd was futile. There were too many bodies, and they were all taller than me. Thinking I would miss the opportunity, I began to look for another option. Certainly there was a cart or a porch I could stand on to see and be seen. *I don't know who is coming, but I am not going to miss this opportunity.* Scanning the streets, I found nothing except a sycamore tree with branches low enough for me to climb. The only opportunity to see over the wall of human flesh between me and the road was a tree. I thought, *There has to be another way. I can't be climbing trees in front of all these taxpayers. I will ruin my reputation; it will make me a laughing stock if anyone sees me. Maybe I should ask someone who is coming before I risk my stature in the community.* "Excuse me, friend, who is coming that would cause such a stir?"

"Jesus is coming! The One who heals the sick and raises the dead!"

Jesus? I thought. *He was the "important one" coming? Why would so many want to see Him?* I had heard that He was as poor as the village He came from and that He lived on the streets unless people opened their homes to Him. *What could He have to offer so many people?* I had even heard that He had to borrow from His disciples to pay His taxes. This all seemed so fishy that I decided to risk it and climb the tree. I figured I could conceal myself in the branches and still see what this Jesus of Nazareth was all about.

As I settled into a comfortable spot, I could see Him coming. I thought, *What's the big deal? He wears cheap clothes; there are no blind seeing, no lame walking. Where are the dead raising...?* While I was trying to find a reason for being there, I realized He was walking toward my tree. *Oh no, He will expose me for sure. Well, maybe He hasn't noticed me...*

Then Jesus said, "Zacchaeus, hurry down from there. I am going to your house today." I didn't say a word, but climbed down and walked with Him to my house. As we were walking, I was wondering how He could have known my name and why He would want to come to my house. Questions seemed to fly through my head from every direction like bats from a cave.

When we arrived at the house, several people yelled, "Look, Jesus is going into the home of a scumbag tax collector." Though He had to have heard them, Jesus kept right on walking into the house without even acknowledging their presence. I had the servants rush together a meal, and I sat Him at the place of honor at the table.

It was there, for the first time, that I saw Him, really saw Him. When I looked into His eyes, it was like He was reading my life story. I could tell He not only knew my name, but He also knew my history, and yet, as He looked at me there was no judgment, no condemnation. He wasn't looking down on me, but rather looking into me and calling out for me as if I was drowning and He was the lifeguard. The longer I looked, the more love I felt pouring from Him. Something was happening inside of me. I knew that what my life had consisted of was worthless, and I knew that it had to change.

Sitting there, I felt the selfish emptiness of my life beginning to be filled. It was as if a well had been dug and there had finally been a breakthrough to the fresh springs. I jumped to my feet and proclaimed, "I will give half of all I own to the poor, and if I have cheated anyone, I will repay them four times what I took."

It was out even before I realized it. *If I had cheated? Who was I kidding? There was hardly anyone I hadn't cheated.* But even the sound of it coming from my mouth felt good, and I meant it. I realized Jesus loved me exactly where I was, but something I saw in His eyes also let me know He loved me too much to leave me there. I wanted to serve Him.

After that, Jesus said, "Salvation has come to this house today. These are the people I have come to seek out and save." I was glad the Seeker had brought salvation to my house that day.

Points to Ponder

1. Zacchaeus was desperate enough for Jesus to risk
    his reputation. In what ways have you risked your
    reputation in order to see Jesus?

2. What are you seeking right now? What might
    Jesus say in response to your need?

3. Have there been times in your life when you were
    dishonest and had to go back, like Zacchaeus, to
    make things right? What happened?

4. What do you think Jesus meant when He said
    "These are the people I have come to seek out and
    save"? What sort of people is He looking for?

Chapter Twelve

Step-Dad

Matthew 1:18-25

"**YOU'RE** what?!?" I exclaimed. "How could you do this to me? How could you do this to our families? How could you do this at all?" The words ripped at my soul even as I spoke them.

"You don't understand, Joseph…" Mary began. "The angel said it was God's child."

"Don't bring God into this," I interrupted. "He may strike you dead for blaming Him for your indiscretion."

Mary tried again, "Joseph, please let me tell you the whole story." Mary began an unbelievable story about how an angel came to her, saying she was going to be made pregnant by God and that the child was to be the long awaited Messiah. I was angry and hurt all at the same time, but I let her finish. I was not convinced. I loved Mary so much and thought the feeling was mutual. Even though our parents had arranged our marriage, I had grown to love her as if I had chosen her myself. It was a match made in Heaven, or so I thought until now.

This was more than I could comprehend. I knew in my heart she was a good girl, but she would not have been the first "good girl" to go bad. What about our families? All this would shame them. Our little town was full of gossips on the prowl for tidbits of juicy news to regurgitate to itching ears. If this got out, as it was sure to, the families would be ruined. They may have to move to another town and start over. Finally, it was more than I could take. I had to get out of there and think.

What should I do? The law says I can reject her as my wife and walk away from any responsibility. But I love her; my family loves her. I can't do that to her no matter how irresponsible she has been. I could send her away until the baby is born. No, that would merely delay the shame. Everyone would know. I can't marry her. She could never be trusted. I'll just end the engagement privately and deal with whatever comes. If anyone asks why, I'll just say I realized it would be a mistake and let the chips fall where they may. I'll keep the truth to myself and give Mary the best chance of a normal life. But, I can't be the father of a bastard child!

Those were my thoughts that night. Though we had not consummated the marriage yet, we were the same as married.

I had spent the last year preparing a place for us to live. That night as I was sleeping, my dilemma changed. In the middle of the night I had a dream, no, a visitation. An angel came to me and told me that everything Mary had said was true and that I should not be afraid to take Mary as my wife.

This child truly was from God and would save His people from their sins. Then he reminded me of what the prophet Isaiah had said hundreds of years before, "A virgin will be pregnant; she will have a son and His name will be Immanuel, which means, 'God is with us.'" When I woke up, I knew it was right and not some bad falafel I had had the night before! Sure there were some questions about the future, but I had no doubt about the angel's story or Mary's story. I had to marry her now and raise God's child as my own.

It wasn't long until everyone knew about the upcoming event. Rumors and gossip hit the fan. Everywhere we went people would look and whisper. You could tell what they were saying. Mary never seemed to let it bother her. If she was bothered, I couldn't tell, and she never said.

But for me, it was a different story. I have to admit, it had been a long time since the visitation, and the promise of that night wore thin several times. It wasn't doubt in God's ability to do the miracle, but rather doubt that Mary was the virgin foretold in the prophets. Were we really the ones chosen to raise the Son of God? The thought that God would choose a nobody carpenter from a tiny nothing town to raise the Messiah was a hard pill to swallow, at least for me.

Nine months can be an eternity in this situation. Just when it seemed it would be over and we could get on with our lives together, we got "the letter"—stating we had to make a 70-mile trip on the unforgiving back of a donkey to Bethlehem for a government census. What bad timing! The baby was almost due, and the last thing Mary wanted to do was ride that donkey, much less for the distance we had to go. But, we had no choice. Caesar called and we had to respond so we packed our belongings and headed for Bethlehem.

The trip was everything I thought it would be—hard! Poor Mary, she had to be so miserable and uncomfortable on the back of that donkey. She never complained, even though she was in the last stage of the pregnancy. Then, when we arrived in Bethlehem, it was so full that there were no rooms available. People had poured in from everywhere and filled not only the inns, but the private homes as well. Then in the search for a place in a filled up world, it happened. Mary's water broke and the labor pains began. There we were, away from home with no midwife to help with the delivery and not even a decent room for Mary to lie down in. I had to do something.

We reached the last inn on the last street; there had to be someplace there. Knocking at the door, I heard a displeased, gruff voice through the door, "Go away! There are no more rooms, nothing available!" I continued knocking until the innkeeper came to the door. The door flew open, revealing a small man with an inflamed, red-faced temper. "I said, go away! I cannot help you!" he said.

"Sir, you don't understand. My wife is about to have our first baby. Certainly there is something you can offer us. It can be anything to get us out of the cold, damp night air. Please!"

Something I said seemed to spark a new thought and he said, "There is a stable out back. Not too clean, but it will be a roof over your head. You can bed down there for the night, and maybe something will open up tomorrow."

I thanked him, but when I saw the stable, I thought my thanks seemed a bit premature. I don't know what I expected; the stable was no different than any I had ever seen. Stinking animals and what stinking animals do was all over. There was only one stall left between an old, broken-down donkey and what looked to be the inn's source of milk. Seeing the cow and her surroundings kept me drinking water for the duration of our stay. I thought, *God, this is where You have chosen for Your Son to be born? I think with Your pull and influence, You could have arranged for at least a room fit for humans.* I hadn't expected a palace, but something above the level of this muck and mire would have been nice.

Her words yanked me from my disgust back to the reality of the moment, "Joseph, it's time!" The baby didn't care about the surroundings; He was coming on His schedule, not ours. I took the blankets we had and made a makeshift bed out of the cleanest straw I could find, then Mary lay down and gave birth to "the Son of God"! Even the thought of it was still hard to digest until I saw Him.

When I saw Him, all of my doubts and fears seemed to fade away. I was caught in that world of new parenting—a place so far from reality, a bubble made for mom, baby, and dad. *He is beautiful. I know everyone says that about their child, but He is the most beautiful baby I have ever seen.* Just then the angel's visitation came back to me like it was yesterday, "a virgin will conceive and bring forth a Son, and You will call Him Jesus."

Later that night, shepherds came to see him. When I asked how they knew to come and look for the child, they told me of another visitation by angels. This time the whole sky was filled with them, and they were praising God and saying that a Savior was born in Bethlehem. I knew before that night that He was special, but when I *saw* Him, I knew something had changed. He was no longer a promise to come, but rather a promise fulfilled. This promise was for Mary, for me, and for anyone who would truly *see* Him!

Points to Ponder

1. Has someone ever told you something that God did or said that seemed absolutely unbelievable, but later you found out it was really true? How did you respond?

2. Jesus was adopted by an earthly father (Joseph) so that we could be adopted by our heavenly Father. What is special about our identity as adopted children? How does it make you feel to know that God chose *you?*

3. Think of the scorn that Joseph and Mary faced for their obedience. Have you ever faced criticism or persecution for being a carrier of the promise? What happened?

4. What do you think may have been God's purpose for having Jesus be born in such lowly and inconvenient circumstances? How might this apply to your life?

Chapter Thirteen

High Dollar Working Girl

Luke 7:36-50

*W*HAT *a way to make a living! My only asset was my body and my tantalizing ways. So far it had paid the bills, but at what cost? How many more beatings at the hands of men out of control would I endure? How many more diseases would I fight through?* Sleepless nights meant business was booming. But after dark, nothing good happened. It seemed the cover of darkness was a playground for the evil of the day. All I had were hopeless days; I was trapped in a prison of my own making. Excuses abounded, but the decisions that had brought me to this place were mine. *I'll just have to live with them.*

"Samaritan Slut!" was what the townspeople called me. Which was worse? *Samaritan* separated me from the two nations of my origin. *Slut* separated me from the rest of the world until nightfall. Then every nation took its fill, as long as the money was there. *All cats are gray in the dark,* I thought. *Used and abused for their particular impulse.* It was a wretched existence, a miserable life with no hope! Escape was something only death offered. There was no chance for advancement, no opportunity for a change. My talents and gifts had limited my prospects. *But I am good at what I do.*

Compared to the others on my street, I had quite a reputation. Men from all over brought me exotic gifts of jewelry, aromatic oils, perfumes, and fine silks and linens woven by the most skilled artisans of the east. They came in handy when the rent came due or food was needed. There was always someone willing to buy these things, even if from a Samaritan Slut! Granted, I had to sell them for below market price, but I was able to live off of them. *Live? Exist* would be a better word, for it had been years since I had experienced the closest resemblance to life.

I had been plundered and left empty, with nothing more to give but a job by the numbers. What had been an art form had now become painting by numbers, assembly line punching out a product, quantity without quality. The promise of the exciting life, the "do what I want when I want," had become the slave-driving merciless master ruling every facet of my life. The expensive jewelry and exquisite fashion gave a beautiful appearance to the empty vessel I had become. Outside delightful, inside detestable. The blindness of desire had taken me down a road I would not have chosen. *But that is my life.*

"Are you tired, weary? Are you weighted down with the life you have chosen? Come here and let me show you life as it is meant to be lived. Sit with me. Learn what I can teach you. For My way is easy. I will walk you through the tough times and get you through to the finish, and you will be the winner!" I heard the stranger say.

Another snake oil salesman promising what he cannot deliver, I immediately thought. *Or is He?* When I *saw* Him, there was something about Him that drew me closer to listen. He was the first man to gain my attention for anything other than business in years. What was it that pulled me into His circle? It could not have been His looks. He was a rather plain looking man, nothing extraordinary to behold. But His eyes and His voice wrapped themselves around me like a father's loving arms, reassuring me that He cared. I couldn't remember when I had last felt that.

I had other places to go, but I was locked in position listening to the hope in His words. I was comforted by the love pouring from His eyes. Time stopped for me. I was carried away to a peaceful place I had never experienced. Soon it was time for Him to leave so I followed. He walked down the street toward the Temple, and then He was ushered into the house of one of the religious leaders. I wanted to go in also, but knew they would never let me in. *But I must see Jesus!*

What can I do? How can I get in there and see Him? I will see Him. I will hear His words of hope. For the first time in my life, I had hope for a future. I had to let Jesus know how I felt. I wanted to give Him a gift, something that would show Him my feelings and my thoughts. *But will He accept anything from someone like me?* I wondered. *Will He even let me close enough to speak? Will He reject me like the others? What will His response be? It doesn't matter. I have to risk it.*

Running home, I kept thinking, *You are so foolish to think Jesus will accept your gift. He can't afford to be seen with the likes of you,* but something drove me on. I chose the best, most fragrant oil I had and ran back to the Pharisee's home.

Before anyone could stop me, I was at the feet of Jesus. I was weeping, and as I did, my tears fell on Jesus' feet. I began to wipe them away with my hair, to kiss His feet, and to anoint Jesus with the perfume I had brought. He turned my way and allowed me to continue. I was expecting Him at any moment to ask me to leave, but He didn't. He never drew back. He sat there and allowed me to continue in front of the others in the house. I could not help but notice their reaction. They were repulsed by my presence, but Jesus welcomed me. I continued to weep, wipe, kiss, and anoint.

As I did, Jesus turned to His host and said, "Simon, I have something to tell you."

Simon arrogantly responded, "Oh? Tell me."

Jesus continued, "Two men were in debt to a banker. One owed 500 silver pieces, the other 50. Neither of them could pay up, and so the banker canceled both debts. Which of the two would be more grateful?"

Simon answered, "I suppose the one who was forgiven the most."

"That's right," said Jesus. Then turning to me, but speaking to Simon, He said, "Do you see this woman? I came to your home; you provided no water for My feet, but she rained tears on My feet and dried them with her hair. You gave me no greeting, but from the time I arrived, she hasn't quit kissing My feet. You provided nothing for freshening up, but she has soothed My feet with perfume. Impressive, isn't it? She was forgiven many, many sins, and so she is very, very grateful. If the forgiveness is minimal, the gratitude is minimal." Then He turned to me and said, "I forgive your sins."

That set the dinner guests talking behind His back. "Who does He think He is, forgiving sins!"

He ignored them and said to me, "Your faith has saved you. Go in peace."

Peace overwhelmed me! I was as light as a feather. It was as if the weight of my life was lifted and I could walk again. I had seen Him for who He was, and when I *saw* Him, my life was changed. I believed and went to Jesus and gave Him what I had, and He accepted me where I was, but He loved me too much to leave me there.

Points to Ponder

1. Do you feel tired and weary with life? Have you ever experienced the lightness of peace in Jesus? How has it changed you?

2. The prostitute was so grateful that she would do anything to get to Jesus. Have you ever felt that way? What did you do in response?

3. What significance might be attached to the fact that the woman took one of the gifts she had received in her profession and used it to worship Jesus?

4. How do you think the woman felt when Jesus did not push her away (though she was unworthy), but received her worship in front of so many onlookers? Have you ever felt the acceptance of Christ like that? How did it affect you?

Chapter Fourteen

Morticia

John 12:1-8

"THAT perfume is worth a year's wage. It should have been sold and the money given to the poor," he shouted. He was speaking of the perfume I had just poured over Jesus as a gift of my love. I was compelled to do it. It was as if I was no longer in control, but my love for the Master had driven me to spill this precious oil out as an offering and a sign of my endless love and devotion. There was no doubt it was an expensive gift for it would have cost the average man a year of his life to purchase it. It was my only thing of value, so I gave it. Why would I do such a thing? Why would I take my savings, my future, and waste it in such a way? Let me explain why I was compelled to offer it freely. That is the real story here.

I had spent the better part of my life controlled, chained to an indescribable ugliness. Choosing to go my own way, walking my own path, determining my own destiny, had led me to him—this entity of disaster. It had been a party turned prison, and I exchanged my faux freedom for exposed slavery. He had been alone in the beginning, but soon made room for his friends, and six others moved in to share his new found territory.

I had decided I was going to decide my fate. I had wanted to move out from under any authority and do my own thing. The society I had been born into oppressed women and gave men the place of honor. We were to walk ten steps behind them, bow and scrape to them, serve them as slaves with no reward or praise. But I knew women who were "in charge." They had made a business of it and seemed to have all they could ever want or need. Sure their profession was looked down on, but what was the difference? I could be despised and broke, or I could be thought of as less than human and have all I could ever desire. You make the choice. I did, and that was when it began.

What a life! I became a welcomed and invited guest to the parties that had previously been off limits. I never knew that people lived this way. *Where did all the money come from?* I wondered. I really didn't care as long as they paid my price. I had been blessed with beauty so I took my only asset and parlayed myself quite a nest egg. The gifts from my clients flowed to me like a natural spring until "they" showed up. I would be in the middle of one of the wild parties, and these uninvited tenants of mine would throw me to the floor, a contorted, writhing mess of humanity. It was a real downer to the parties, and soon I was off the guest lists.

Before long, the nest egg had to be cracked and eaten. The only thing I held onto was one bottle of expensive perfume. I took it to my sister and asked her to keep it for me. "Don't give it to me under any circumstances," I told her. I was not welcome anywhere. Unable to peddle my wares, I soon took up residence in the streets, sleeping where I could, when I could, when my dark residents of disaster would allow it. They were in total control. I could do nothing without their approval. I had become a slave.

The very thing I had been running from was the very thing I had become. I was thought of as crazy, a wild woman, demon possessed. The townspeople were right about one thing. I was possessed by a force that controlled my every action. I could think for myself, but I was unable to act on those thoughts. It was almost like I was outside my body watching this person I recognized, but did not know. They lived inside me, and I had no way to evict them. Then it happened! A miracle! I met the Master!

I was walking down the street in a daze when they threw me to the ground with a force stronger than I had ever felt. The blood began to flow from both the newest wounds and the broken scabs of the unhealed wounds. As I tried to regain what little control I had to stand up, they called a council and spoke up. "Why are you troubling us, Son of David?"

They spoke with a trembling voice of fear that I had never heard before. They had spoken before, but always with an authority that would strike fear in the hearts of the hearers, but this time there was something so strikingly different; I could almost see them cowering like children behind a mother's leg. I would have laughed had the pain not been so excruciating. *Why are they afraid? Who is it that commands even their respect and fear?* Then I heard His voice.

"Come out of her and set her free!"

The unwanted strangers racked me with pain once more, and I collapsed to the ground. Then the pain was washed away by a honeyed peace that started at my head and poured over my being, replacing the chains of bitterness and hate with the sweetness of freedom. I realized it was real when I was able to think clearly for the first time in years. All the noise, all the voices were silent, gone! Unable to speak, I looked for the One who had freed me.

Then I saw Him! *A man? Or is He? Oppression from men drove me away, and now a man has loosed my chains and let me go? Who is this man? Why did He help me?* All the questions left me confused. Then I looked into His eyes. I saw, for the first time in my life, the love I had been searching for. I had no more questions. I only knew I was free and I owed Him, Jesus, everything. He went with me to meet my brother and sister. They invited Him into their home and hearts.

Since that time we have spent many days with Jesus, and one day I was compelled once more by a power greater than my own. What would make me spill out my pension for old age? It was the love I have for Him. What's the difference? I now have the option, the ability to love, and that came when I *saw* Him for the first time! And He accepted the gift as He had accepted me, without condition. That day I saw Him again in a new light.

Points to Ponder

1. Have you ever been controlled by or addicted to something? Have you found freedom? How?

2. What do we learn about the Father's heart through the fact that He used the very place of offense in the woman's life (hurt from men) to bring her healing (through a man)? What areas in your life might need this sort of healing?

3. The woman chose to give Jesus her most valuable possession because of her great love for Him. What valuable part of your life can you give to Him as an act of worship?

4. Someone questioned the wisdom of her gift, saying that the money could have been used for better things. What attitude does this convey? When have you been guilty of thinking that some need in your life was more important than wholehearted worship?

Chapter Fifteen

Hired Gun

Acts 9:1-20

I *can't believe what he said! My own mentor saying we need to be tolerant, just when we were about to get rid of these wild-eyed fanatics who would destroy the purity of our religion and replace it with some bastardized imposter. What is the world coming to?* I thought. We had just caught some of Jesus' disciples preaching the erroneous Gospel that "the only way to Heaven was through Jesus" and that He was "the Messiah sent to save the world."

All we needed was a majority vote and they could be done away with. But *no!* Gamaliel, my own teacher, said, "Be tolerant. If they are wrong, they will burn out. If they are right, there is nothing we can do to stop them or their message because it is God's power behind them." The council agreed and let them go with a stern warning. *What a waste of breath!* No sooner had we let them go then the disciples returned to the streets and started saying the same things.

I had listened to all I was going to tolerate when Stephen, one of the more zealous ones, began to preach—right out on the streets in front of the temple. Stephen was unstoppable. People listened everywhere he went and believed his lies. He had to be silenced. I organized several of my fellow students to bring formal charges against him before the high priests and the Sanhedrin. "Stephen is spreading slanderous words against Moses, the law, and the Holy One of Israel," I stated forcefully. I continued with my argument of how this type of rabble would be the demise of our faith, and it worked.

They dragged Stephen before the court, and after he had his say the high priest and the council became so angry they jumped on him, like a duck on a June bug, threw him out of the city, and stoned him to death. I was proud to be there, and even held their coats while they chucked the rocks. It was a bit unnerving when Stephen looked to the sky and mumbled something about forgiving us of our sin, and then he asked Jesus to "receive his spirit." The look on his face was not the face of the executed, but rather the exonerated—but he was dead! *No matter what he looked like, it was done, and I now had helped turn the tide away from heresy to purity.*

I was so excited by my accomplishment. I knew God had to be excited as well as pleased by my faithfulness to protect the truth—His truth. I thought, *I am just what God needs, someone with the ability to motivate the normally passive to action. The high council had taken a few steps backward since they got rid of that carpenter from Nazareth. They had taken the "Gamaliel Road" of tolerance—until today.* I felt so proud; I had been the catalyst to move them off center.

All I could think about was what to do next to further my agenda. *Now is the time! Strike while the iron is hot!* I went to the high priest and convinced him to give me the authority to carry out my plan to save the religion. He issued me letters giving me the right to arrest and bring back to Jerusalem, those "heretics of the faith." Success!

I hit the ground running. Jerusalem first, then Judea, then Samaria, then the world; I was determined to defeat this new Way that had invaded our truth. I went house to house, chains in hand, sending mothers, fathers, sons, and daughters to prison. People scattered like water from a stomped puddle. They headed out of town, and I realized I would have to take this show on the road soon. I then got the authority to go to Damascus. I packed a donkey, hired some henchmen, and headed out. *I have an appointment with destiny in Damascus,* I thought. I had no idea!

It was several hard days of riding and living out in the elements to make it to Damascus. It was a big change compared to the comforts of home. *A roof over my head, a soft bed, and a relative life of leisure are worth giving up,* I told myself. *It is a small sacrifice for such a worthy cause.*

It was the third night on the trail when the nightmares started robbing me of what little rest could be had on the hard, dusty ground of the Cesarean wilderness. These were not normal childhood dreams. They were scenes from my life—the stoning of Stephen, the scourgings of my enemies, me banging on doors in Jerusalem and dragging people to prison—but each had the same twist at the end that would wake me in a sweat. Every time I looked at the faces of the accused, it was the same face. It was a face I had never seen, but it was the same person each time. *Who is He? What do the dreams mean? Are they some kind of message, or have I had too many spices on this camp food we have been eating?* Each morning brought a new day, each night the same nightmares.

The sixth day dawned. The gray mist of morning was giving way to the golden sunrise as I awoke from another restless night. With dampened zeal, we loaded up to move out. It seemed even the animals were slower. It didn't matter for the end of the day would find me in a comfortable inn. *Then I can rest up to prepare for the work—no, the mission—I was sent here to accomplish.* Pushing to make Damascus before nightfall meant not stopping for anything. No lunch, no rest stops. I was not going to spend another night on the trail. The sun was high and bright and beginning to bake everything around us. My mind was on the nightmares and what they could possibly mean when *it* happened.

A light, brighter than the noonday sun, came beaming down on me and knocked me off my horse and to the ground. The light was all around. There were no shadows anywhere. I was in the midst of a power I had never experienced before. As I was trying to regain my composure, I heard a voice addressing me, saying, "Saul, why are you persecuting Me?"

I looked toward the voice, and I saw Him—the face in my dreams. My only answer came out, "Who are You?"

"I am Jesus who you are persecuting. It is hard for you to fight your conscience," He answered.

Jesus? He said "Jesus," the One I have been persecuting? We had never met before, but I knew it was Him, Jesus, the One who had been crucified. His disciples preached that He had risen from the grave, but I had never met Him or anyone who had seen Him after the cross. *He is Jesus!* I knew at that moment that He was there talking with me.

Fear overcame me. Every joint in my frame seemed to give way, and every muscle began to shake and twitch. All I could do was ask Him, "Lord, what do You want me to do?" (Yes, I called Him Lord; at that moment, He was the master of my very life. He clearly had the power to do with me what He wished.)

He told me to go into the city. There, He said, I would be told what to do. And as suddenly as He had appeared, He was gone—and so was my sight. My encounter with Jesus had blinded my physical eyes, but I had a feeling the eyes that had been blinded for years were about to receive the sight that really mattered.

Those who were with me had seen the light and heard the noise, but had not understood what was said. They came to my aid when they realized the light had blinded me. I could see nothing so they led me to Damascus. For three days, I sat in dark silence, eating and drinking nothing.

My time was spent in seeing with new eyes, considering the truth that had been right under my nose, but that I had refused to see. For the first time in all my religious life, I realized the Messiah had come. *His name is Jesus. He is who He said He is! I was persecuting Him by persecuting His followers. Instead of destroying me, which would have been no challenge for Him, He had rescued me, saved me from myself.*

I hardly noticed when Ananias arrived. He told the others there that Jesus had come to him and told him to come to me, lay hands on me, and pray that I might receive my sight. When he did, something like fish scales fell from my eyes and I could see again, but for the first time in my life I also had *sight!* In a blinding ray of light, I received my sight when I saw Him.

Points to Ponder

1. Have you, like Saul, ever been so certain you knew the truth that you couldn't see what God was doing? How did Jesus help you see the truth?

2. What attitude do you have toward people who believe differently than you? How does it compare to Saul's attitude?

3. What was Jesus' response to Saul's self-righteousness? How does it compare to His response to those who were aware of their brokenness and sin?

4. Saul was zealous, but for the wrong cause. When he saw Jesus, his zeal was transferred to a righteous purpose and used to change the world. In what areas of your life has Jesus redeemed personality traits or interests for His glory? What does this show you about His love for you?

Chapter Sixteen

Hopeless

Mark 5:25-34

I was wealthy at one time. Fact was, I had more than enough to care for my needs. I was self-sufficient, my own person. No one needed to support me, at least not until the problems hit like a ton of bricks. I could not have seen it coming nor could I have prepared for it. At first my monthly "ordeal" lengthened in time, then in intensity. Before long, it had turned into a daily, weakening flow of life. The embarrassment was only overshadowed by the weakness this malady had brought. I was declared "unclean" by the leaders of the temple. They made me an outcast when it continued. At a time when I needed the comfort of friends and family, I was declared an "untouchable" and sentenced to a life outside my circle of solace.

The security I had dwindled with every new remedy attempt that came along. It seemed the word had gotten out. I was sick and well off. Plenty of money and little hope are fertile soil for seeds of quackery and con. One, two, five, ten years passed. No help could be found. There was always the "newest thing" until my purse was empty. *Funny,* I thought, *how help is always available for a price, but let the funds dry up and, "I am sorry. There is nothing else we can do."* Weak from my plight, alone in my circumstance, stuck in a disheartening maze of apprehension, I wondered, *What can I do? Where can I go? Nothing has helped. No one will help...*

One day, while walking through town, I found a place to rest for a moment away from the crowd in the streets. It was the only way to have any semblance of peace. When anyone saw me, they would yell, "Unclean, unclean" and kick dust toward me as a symbol of the fact that they wanted nothing to do with the likes of me. I had been cursed by something, and they did not want it to rub off on them. I was resting and hoping for enough strength to continue in my search for food and shelter when I heard the clamor of the multitude gathering at the shore of Galilee. A crowd was unusual for this time of day. Most had left the sea for the markets to peddle their goods, but this day it was different. Something held this crowd's attention, and they were headed my way. Then I saw Him!

Jesus, the Rabbi from Nazareth, was coming my way. I had heard of Him before, but that day was the first time I had seen Him. Something about Him compelled me to reach Him even though touching Him would be wrong. I knew what the law said. No one in my condition was to touch a Rabbi and make him unclean. It was punishable by death if someone did it on purpose. The crowd was thick and congested. *Why even try to fight through?* was my first thought, but something inside me kept saying, *If I can just get to Him, He can help.*

The energy that surged through my body and the thoughts I was having were unbelievable. Before I saw Him, I was sure all the promises had been exhausted, every hope spent, just like my last coins. With every new physician had come an empty, unfulfilled promise of healing. Yet, when I saw Him, something rose up on the inside of me. *I must reach Him, but how do I get through the thronging mass of humanity? Was this newfound strength enough? Could I make it close enough for Him to see me?* Doubts and questions flooded my mind, but nothing was going to deter me. *I will make it!*

The crowd never even noticed who I was. They were pressing to see Him as well. As I was pushing through, the strain was almost more than I could bear. My heart was pounding through my chest. The pain, as my lungs struggled to take in air, caused me to stumble. As I was falling, everything seemed to go into slow motion. I was almost to Him. *One more step and I can reach Him. One more moment and He will be out of reach for good.* I pushed with all available strength in one last attempt to touch Him. *If I can just touch the hem of His coat, I will be healed,* I thought. I pushed, pushed hard, and as I hit the ground in a puff of dust, my hand brushed the last thread of the last chance I had. Everything went quiet.

Everything was still. All of existence seemed to come to a halt. The Keeper of time inspected every moment as if searching for its favorite. Lying there, I tried to understand what was happening as a gentle warming began in my hand and coursed through my weakened form. The heat flushed over my body, bringing life and strength. Where death had ruled as king, *life* was banishing him to the abyss. The flow, which had been my curse, was dammed and stopped. The life that had been draining from my being was now coursing on its right path. Muscles weak and frail regained strength and vitality that I hadn't felt in years, if ever. My joy was uncontrollable until I heard His voice, "Who touched me?"

I was the culprit, but how could He know with so many crowding in to touch Him. Even His disciples asked the same question. He answered, "Someone touched Me, and I felt the healing power leave Me!"

I had taken a healing and not paid for it. I was unworthy to receive such a gift. *If I reveal myself, will He reject me and take it back? Will He have me stoned according to the law? If I don't reveal myself, will I lose the healing anyway?* I knew it was only a matter of time until He found me, so I cried out, "I touched You because I believed if I could touch You I could be healed. As sure as I am here right now, as soon as I touched your coat I was healed. I have been sick for 12 years, and I spent all my wealth on doctors who couldn't help me. But today You healed me as I touched You."

I knelt there, hoping He would not take away the gift I had just received. No, I hadn't asked; I only believed. I would have asked if I had had enough strength to press through the crowd. As I was putting together a good reason for keeping the healing, He surprised me with His words "Daughter…"

Wait, I thought, *Did He call me daughter? Not woman, not lady, but daughter?*

He continued, "…be happy. Your faith has made you well. Go in peace."

He didn't have to tell me to be happy. Joy flooded my soul, and I knew this was my miracle. "Go in peace," He said. This was a peace that settled all my issues. What if I hadn't pressed in? What if I hadn't reached out? But I did, and when I saw Him, that was it! I received all I needed. Suddenly I had a future bright, a hope restored; I was dreaming again just because I saw Him!

Points to Ponder

1. What's the difference between the Old Testament ideals of clean/unclean and the way Jesus responded to the sick woman? How might this impact the way you treat others?

2. Have you ever felt like people only cared about you because of what you could give them or do for them? What did Jesus do to show that His love is different?

3. Jesus didn't care that the woman was "unclean" or that she didn't ask permission. What characteristic mattered most to Him?

4. What enabled the woman to overcome her limitations in order to touch Jesus? How might this enable you to overcome the things in your life that may be holding you back?

Chapter Seventeen

Silent One

Mark 7:32-37

THE silence screamed miserably. The sounds of the market were foreign to me. I could smell the fresh fruits and vegetables, but I could not hear the farmer hocking his goods. Maybe it was a blessing from that perspective, but trying to communicate was a joke. Only those closest to me had learned my crude hand signals, and even they became impatient at times. I tried to speak, but the noises only came out slurred and impeded by lack of experience. How was I to know how to make the right sounds? I had never heard any before.

As a child, I had been rejected by all the neighborhood children, denied entrance into school, and finally left on my own, on the streets to try and scrape together some meager form of existence. Though infrequent, occasionally people would have pity and take me in for a meal or a night's rest. But soon after, when they had fulfilled their compassionate duty, I was back on the streets.

I did have friends, but they were worse off than I was. Blind, crippled, and leprous beggars were my circle of friends. The blind leading the blind, the cripple carrying the cripple, the sick tending the sicker—what a set of circumstances. You can't get water from an empty well, blood from a turnip, or hope from the hopeless. Help was not coming our way; hope had long since left, and happiness was a mythological concept...until one day.

Strangely our number had begun to shrink. First, one of the blind men mysteriously received his sight one morning while begging in front of the temple. That spot was covered with blind guys seeking what he had found. Then there was a group of lepers who had been cleansed. Then, it was my turn.

It had started out like most other days. The sun rose in the east, making its dependable track across the sky. The market had opened as usual with its bustling crowd trying to make their day's purchases and the vendors making their daily wage. I was making my way through the town square when some friends took my attention almost by force. I recognized them as friends only after the shock of realizing that they were all different than the last time I had seen them. One had been blind and now was leading the pack with a sure step instead of a tapping cane. Another, a leper who would have never touched a friend, was now holding my arm with a clean hand with all the fingers. These were the same friends, but they had been changed.

What are we doing? Where are we going? I tried to communicate with them, but they were not distracted by my feeble attempts. They were on a mission, and I was along for the ride. Maybe they had found a magician who could do these types of tricks, changing them from frogs to princes. Or maybe they had found an easy mark to get food and shelter. I had no idea, but I was coming along whether I wanted to or not. When we reached the sea, we saw a great crowd. *What is all the commotion about? Why are all these people at the sea long after the day's catch has been brought in?* I wondered.

Then I saw Him. I had never seen Him before, but they took me right up to Him and began speaking to Him in earnest. I had learned to read lips, and what they were saying confused me. "He is deaf; if You will just touch him, he will be able to hear."

Who is this man who they think can make me hear? In appearance, He was nothing special that people would be drawn to Him. He had no wealth, or at least He didn't show it. He wore the clothes of the common man. He was not a man who would please the ladies' taste either. *What is it about Him that made them bring me to Him?* I couldn't make sense of it.

Just then He took me aside. He said nothing for a moment. Why would He? I could not have heard it if He had. Then He did something that took me by surprise. He stuck His fingers in my ears. Then He spit in His hand and touched it to my tongue. My first response was to draw back and spit in His face. Thoughts raced through my mind, and many could not be expressed without a fight.

Suddenly, my response changed. It would have been normal to be repulsed, but His eyes were saying things I thought I was imagining. They were saying, "Only believe. I am about to give you a gift to change your life for eternity." He looked away toward Heaven and sighed. Just as I began to think, *He has given up, I am a hopeless case,* I heard, "Be opened." I heard, "Be opened." *I heard!* For the first time in my life, I heard with my ears. I was shocked and amazed. I was so filled with joy, I began to shout. What had been garbled, indistinguishable noise became clear words of praise for the One who had touched me. He had opened my ears and given me clear speech.

My friends were as amazed as I was. I grabbed the hand of my previously leprous friend, the hand that had fallen off months ago, and we began to dance around in the streets shouting the praise of the Healer. Who was He? He was Jesus, the carpenter from Nazareth! But He was not restoring works in wood; rather He was building lives with human material. He can do the same for anyone. I am so glad I had friends who cared enough to take me to Him. When I saw Him, my life changed forever.

Points to Ponder

1. Have you ever known someone who is deaf? Imagine the sort of communication isolation they experience. What do you think the deaf man felt when Jesus healed him?

2. When Jesus put His fingers in the man's ears and His spit on his tongue, it offended him. Can you think of times when God's work in your life initially offended you? How did you respond?

3. What about Jesus turned the deaf man's offense into openness? What can you learn from this in regard to your ministry to others?

4. If the deaf man also symbolizes those who are spiritually deaf, what would his friends symbolize? What implications could that metaphor have for your life?

Chapter Eighteen

Subletter, No More Vacancy

John 20:1-18

*W*HERE *have they taken Him? Why have they taken Him? Haven't they had their way with Him enough? Are they going to exploit His body by desecrating it more, as if that is possible?*

I had come to anoint His body with oils and perfumes and finish the burial preparations that had been suspended because of the lateness of the hour before Sabbath. The mist of the morning was eerily refreshing as it rose from the floor of the garden. It was a stark contrast to the agony of the past few days and the gruesomeness of this morning's job that lay ahead of me.

I wondered if I would recognize Him after the repugnance of the cross. I had been there when they removed Him and was aghast to see the form that had been my friend. I had to turn away from the terror that was His body. But I would not turn away from this morning's task. It would be the last act of love I could give to the One who had changed my life forever, the One who delivered me from the prison that I called life before He came along.

I had been raised in a city called Magdala on the Sea of Galilee. It was a fishing town full of the things that fill fishing towns: fishermen, fish markets, fish nets, fish, fish, fish! Everything I owned from my earliest recollection smelled like fish. It wasn't so bad as a child; in fact, I loved the sea. We used to play as children along the shore. The lapping waves were always refreshing to our feet, hot and tired from walking the dusty streets of Magdala.

My parents had tried to "raise me right," but the dye never set in the fabric of my soul. I had to travel another road, different from my heritage. I rebelled as some young people do, but the result was different from any I had ever seen.

The fortune-tellers and diviners always held my attention. I had always wondered what it would be like to know the future. I had always been told that they were all fakes, but when I went to them, they made sense, and some of what they foretold came true. Fascination soon turned to obsession as I began to move toward my new future, much to the regret of my parents. *But what do they know?* I reasoned. *They have been stuck in their rut for years with no hope or desire to get out.* I was determined to never be caught in their rut. Little did I know that I was digging my own, palm by palm.

I don't remember when the first one showed up and took residence. He was probably a welcomed guest to accomplish part of this ill-advised dream I had of emancipation from my lame heritage in Magdala, the fishing town. I now see that the fish had been hooked, and I was that catch being drawn in by an expert fisherman with my demise in his plans. After he had firm root, he invited six more of his friends over, and I was subletting. My house, my soul, had been subdivided and leased to the most unwanted tenants, but I had no authority to evict them. I was stuck with them and had arranged my life to accommodate them the best I knew how. It was crazy, but they had taken over, and I was at their beck and call to do their bidding. It was my house, but I had relinquished my rights of occupancy completely. I was no longer the master of the castle; they were. That was, until I saw Him.

He was walking along the shore of the Sea of Galilee with His disciples when I saw Him for the first time. I turned and ran uncontrollably from His sight without knowing why. It was like being driven by a fear that I had never felt before. *Why am I afraid of this man by the sea? What sent me running? Why is it, when I was out of His sight, that the fear subsided and the urge to run ceased?* I was no longer in control of my body, but I often was able to have a clear thought, and that was when I realized that they had made me run—the subletters. *Why are they afraid of Him?* I wondered. *If they are so afraid that they have to run, maybe I should check Him out. He may have power over them that I do not.*

I found myself looking for Him, seeking to meet this man from whom I had been driven by my "tenants." When I found Him, they threw me to the ground with a vengeance. I had to be a sight because people ran in fear as I writhed on the ground. It was a failed plan if they had wanted to get rid of Jesus, for when He saw me and the state that I was in, rather than being chased away, He was drawn to me. The subletters had made their final mistake.

Jesus came over to where I was and spoke, "Come out of her!"

Peace… calm…rest, all in a moment. It came so fast, and they were gone so quickly that I wondered if it had all been a dream. A nightmare it had been, but a real one that I had lived with for so long that the reality of the eviction left me speechless. My life had not been my own to command for years, but suddenly I had a newfound control. I was able to function again as a normal human. Then, as quickly as He had freed me, He was gone. He continued on His way, not expecting any payment for His services. I had received the greatest gift I could have ever received, and He had required nothing of me in the form of repayment. *A free gift! I have to repay Him, but how? I will give Him my life!*

That is what I did. I spent the rest of His time here with us following Him, listening to Him, and ministering to Him. As I spent more time with Him, I came to think that

He was the Messiah, the Promised One who would restore the Kingdom of David, our great king. Once again Israel would be all God intended it to be. At least I had believed that until three days before my trip to the tomb—when I saw Him die on Calvary.

Now I was coming to minister to His needs for the last time to show Him my love for the gift He gave me, deliverance. When I arrived at the tomb, it had been opened. I looked inside and the body was gone. *Where is the body of my Deliverer? Who could have done this? Who would have done this? Why would anyone steal the body of a dead man?* I walked outside of the tomb and sat down crying; I had been robbed of the last act of love.

"Woman, why are you weeping?" the gardener asked.

Maybe he saw someone come and take Him. Maybe he can tell me where they took Him so I can go where the body is now. Through my tears and sorrow I said, "Sir, please tell me, where have they taken my Master's body?" The heavy weight of grief kept me from looking up.

"Mary."

I know that voice! "Jesus?" I responded. I turned and grasped ahold of Him as if to say, "You are not getting away this time." It wasn't a dream. I really saw Him and touched Him. I had seen the Deliverer that day on the road to Magdala, but at the tomb I really saw Him, the risen Lord. He had set me free years before, but that day my life was changed anew when I saw Him.

Points to Ponder

1. Have you ever dabbled in the occult? As a result, did you ever experience demonic oppression? Have you found freedom through Jesus? How?

2. Have you had the revelation that Jesus' gift to you is free? How did that impact you?

3. When Mary was delivered from her subletters, she decided to give Jesus her life by following and serving Him. What does giving your life to Jesus look like for you? How has it changed your life?

4. What was the difference in Mary's first revelation of Jesus, when she was delivered, and her second revelation, after His resurrection? How might this bring greater revelation of Jesus to your life?

Chapter Nineteen

Water Girl

John 4:4-42

"THE hottest part of the day and I have to walk a mile to get water," I thought out loud, as if scolding would change the facts.

Why did I wait until then instead of going earlier when everyone else did? The other ladies of Sychar went at first light during the cool of the day. Why not me? I had at first, but the ridicule I received from the ladies there had been more than I could bear. They would chide me with, "Women of her type will spoil the well," and "She should be able to pay someone to carry her water with the thriving business she has."

The verbal jabs had often progressed to corporal attacks. I was a Samaritan of Samaritans. Not only judged for my race, I was despised by my own ethnic group because of the life I had chosen. Of course, I hadn't started out that way. The plan had not been to become what I was. Life had just dealt me a bum hand, and I had played the cards the best I knew how.

With my first husband gone, what was I to do? Find another? But who would have me? Feeling less than worthy, I took the first offer that came along. He proved to be the wrong choice, and then came husband number three. I refer to him as Erron, short for "erroneous selection"; and then there was husband number four, "ill-advised mistake." Husband number five was "Mr. Wright"—right over here, right over there, right everywhere but never right here. *I won't make the same mistake for the sixth time,* I thought to myself. *I am not going to marry. Why, he probably won't be here long anyway.*

I know I looked like a whore to the people of the town; I lived, or rather existed, by animal instinct. Survival instinct had taken hold and made me subservient to its whims and wishes. Avoidance had become the rule of my life—evade the market when busy, circumvent the road when most traveled, stay away from the well except in the heat of the day when no one would be there.

It was another hot Israeli day, and noon meant I must hurry to the well and then return home for other duties. But this day would prove to be different. How many "moments of a lifetime" had I passed up during my life? How was I to recognize them? There was no way to know, but I was about to experience one of those moments that would make a difference of a lifetime—and eternity.

As I approached the well, I saw Him. He was a Jew so I just knew I was in for at least a shunning. *Why is He at the well at this time of the day?* It would be my luck that He was some sort of religious wannabe and would take advantage of the opportunity to make an example of me in front of any passersby. I did not know who He was, but I was also not looking for any new friends, certainly none of the Jewish persuasion.

I thought, *Walk slow; maybe He will leave before I get there.* That became increasingly unlikely as the well drew closer and closer. It was almost as if He was waiting for me to get there. He saw me coming. He had plenty of time to move away as I, the scourge of the Jews, approached. I was sure I was in for a spitting or at least a roll of the eyes—*why else is He waiting?*

At the well, I diverted my eyes so as not to stir any disdain that the man was not already prepared to spew. As I raised my water from the well, He spoke, "Please give me a drink."

I was shocked and surprised. Not only had He addressed me and given an order, but He had said *please.* The tone and timbre of His voice was like a soft, gentle rain refreshing the parched ground of my soul. Caught off guard by the gentleness, I retorted from reflex, "You are a Jew! Why do You ask me for a drink?"

I was harsh. Not in response to His request, but rather as a reaction from years of misuse and abuse. I had a sharp tongue, and I was not afraid to use it. But something about this time made me feel wrong. Again, I knew something was different when He responded to my quip.

He stated, "If you knew the gift of God and who it is that asks you for a drink, you would have asked Him and He would have given you living water."

Who are You? I thought, *And what is this gift of God You speak of? And how will You even get any water?* He had neither a pot nor a rope to lower it with. Before I thought, my quick tongue took over, "Sir," I said, "You have nothing to draw with and the well is deep. Where can You get this living water? Are You greater than our father Jacob, who gave us the well and drank from it himself as did also his sons and his flocks and herds?"

For a moment I thought, *I'm amazing! I'm sharp and fast on my feet!* But even as I spoke the words, I felt like I was scolding an innocent man. What had He done but step across the racial lines of prejudice and ask me for a drink? Then He blew me away!

"People soon become thirsty again after drinking this water. But the water I give them takes away thirst altogether. It becomes a perpetual spring, an Artesian well within them, giving them eternal life."

Takes away thirst altogether? Never have to come to the well in the heat of the day? Never have to endure the occasional scoff from a latecomer to the well? I blurted out, "Please sir, give me some of that water! Then I'll never be thirsty again, and I won't have to keep coming here to haul water." The thought was overwhelming and unbelievable.

Then He said, "Go, call your husband and come back."

Call my husband? What does that have to do with the water? Hoping He would move on to giving me this everlasting spring, I replied, "I have no husband."

Have you ever felt like someone set you up? Well, that was how I was feeling right about then because when I said I had no husband this man told me, "You're right! You don't have a husband for you have had five husbands, and you aren't even married to the man you're living with now." I had to change the subject. He was getting too close for comfort. This was no joke, and I had to do something fast so I answered Him with, "Sir, You must be a prophet. So tell me, why is it that You Jews insist that Jerusalem is the only place of worship, while we Samaritans claim it is here at Mount Gerizim, where our ancestors worshiped?"

That's the answer, I thought. *Talk religion. Usually that gets a Jew off any subject. You know how those religious types are—always ready to argue some minor point of the religious law that has little to no application to my life.* Thinking that would be the end of the conversation, I began to make preparations to leave.

Then He came back with, "Believe Me, the time is coming when it will no longer matter whether you worship the
Father here or in Jerusalem. You Samaritans know so little
about the One you worship, while we Jews know all about
Him, for salvation comes through the Jews. But the time is
coming and is already here when true worshipers will worship the Father in spirit and in truth. The Father is looking for anyone who will worship Him that way. For God is
Spirit, so those who worship Him must worship in spirit and
in truth."

It looked like I was in this conversation till the end so
I decided to cut it short. I said, "I know the Messiah will
come, the One who is called Christ. When He comes, He
will explain everything to us."

To that He said, "I am the Messiah! You don't have to
wait any longer or look any further."

What did He just say? I mused a moment and then
responded, "I'm sorry, I thought You said You are the Messiah?" He replied not a word, but looked into my eyes with a
purity that assured me I had heard right, and the beating of
my heart underscored it as truth. *The Messiah is talking with
me, a Samaritan?*

Thrown off balance by the thought, I hardly noticed His
followers coming around until I caught the all too familiar
glares of disapproval. As I was observing their stares, one
of them addressed the man by the well. "Jesus, why are You
talking to her?"

Jesus? Jesus of Nazareth? I had heard of Him. He was the miracle-worker. He had opened blind eyes, set people free from demons that tortured them, made the lame walk, and even raised the dead. Just then, He caught my eye, and I knew—when I saw Him, I would never be the same. I turned and ran into the city telling passersby, "Come see a man who knew all about the things I did, who knows me inside and out. Do you think this could be the Messiah?"

I had left in such a hurry that I had forgotten my water. It didn't matter; I was going to return to hear more from this man, Jesus! But I had to tell others. I had happened upon a great discovery, and I could not keep it to myself. I normally would have taken advantage of the moment and kept valuable information to myself for future gain, but something inside me compelled me to tell all who would listen, to tell them everything I knew.

When I returned, people had streamed out to see Him like a spring deluge. A crowd was sitting at His feet hearing the good news of the Kingdom of God. They all begged Him to stay, and for the next two days He spent His time teaching us things that would change our hearts—new, mysterious things of the Kingdom of Heaven that were so different from anything we had ever heard. For weeks after, people came up to me, as if we were now joined together by some relation that made us family, and said, "Now we believe because we have heard Him ourselves, not just because of what you told us. He is indeed the Savior of the world."

I had spent my whole life ignoring "moments in time" that could have changed me. Instead I went my own way, the way that seemed best to me. And it just about ruined me. But when I saw Him, all of that changed. That "moment in time" changed my eternity.

Points to Ponder

1. In the woman's life, one poor choice led to another until she seemed trapped in her way of life. Have you ever experienced this? What happened?

2. The woman felt like a victim of her circumstances. Are there times when you've felt like a victim? How did her perspective change by the end? What can you learn from her experience?

3. When Jesus tried to minister to her, the woman initially tried to distract Him by starting a religious argument. What did Jesus do to disarm her?

4. After she knew the truth, the woman ran to tell the people who had previously persecuted her. What does this show you about the joy of salvation? In what ways can you grow in your excitement about sharing the good news with everyone?

Chapter Twenty

Hunchback

Luke 13:10-17

EIGHTEEN wretched years, but what can I do? Become bitter and lose any chance of joy? Lose all hope in the pain of this affliction? Or do I continue to do what I know is right and hope that someday I will be healed or delivered? Though it was not easy, I chose the latter because hope allowed me to continue with some semblance of life.

Yes, it was true that people stared at me, and in my neighborhood many thought that I had some kind of evil in my past and that God was making me pay for it. But I knew my God did not take things out on His children. He is a loving God who longs to bless His kids with every kind of good thing. So what if I was bent over like a palm in a hurricane; I was still alive, and I could still function. Many others were not so lucky. I would continue to do what I knew to do in the hope that one day God would do what only He can do, heal me.

When the Sabbath came, I was in the temple. That was where I could be closest to God. It was there that I heard the stories of how He had delivered Israel time and time again from those who would have destroyed them. The Midianites, Amalekites, Perizzites, Canaanites, and many other extinct "ites" had tried, but God had always delivered Israel. No human force was greater than God. Then there were the natural barriers that He overcame. The Red Sea held back its water. The rock in the desert flowed with sweet water. Only God could do that. I knew that my hardship was nothing for God to heal. He had just not done it yet. I decided, if I were to be healed, it would be in the temple, where I was closest to God. It was there I would expect my healing and wait for it to come.

That day was just another day at the temple, and it was crowded. Many had said there would be a special speaker—Jesus. It was the Sabbath, a day of rest and worship. I took my place in the back, away from the discomfort of the ogling of onlookers, and waited for Him to turn up.

His arrival came with no fanfare. In fact, few even noticed His entrance. When Jesus came in, I was shocked by His appearance. He was certainly nothing to look at as far as physical beauty, but there was something about His eyes. They seemed to look through you and see all there was to know about you. I had seen that kind of look before from so many who would blame my malady on my past failures. The priests in the temple often had looked my way with piercing, accusatory gawks, but His eyes were different. They looked right through you, but they never condemned. When His eyes caught yours, they said "Peace, love, joy are all yours for the taking."

I was drawn to Him by some mysterious power, and then He saw me. He had looked my way before, but I knew He was looking at me this time. It was as if He was saying, "Be at peace. You are going to make it. You are going to be whole" without ever saying a word. He had no doubt been drawn to me by the deformity my body had become. I looked like I was eternally caught between getting up and getting down, no matter what I did. *Is He judging me like all the rest? Does He wonder what sin I committed to deserve such trial?* Before I could come to a conclusion, He said, "Woman, you're free!"

He laid His hands on me, and suddenly I was standing straight and tall, giving glory to God. I was thrilled, ecstatic, over the moon emotional, for I had received what I had longed for. I had been in the right place at the right time, and He had seen me and healed me. All the years of anguish and desolation melted away, a faint memory compared to the rapture of this new body I had been given.

The local Jewish leader in charge of the synagogue was very angry about it because Jesus had healed me on the

Sabbath day. "There are six days of the week to work," he shouted to the crowd. "Those are the days to come for healing, not on the Sabbath!"

But Jesus replied, "You hypocrite! You work on the Sabbath! Don't you untie your cattle from their stalls on the Sabbath and lead them out for water? And is it wrong for Me, just because it is the Sabbath day, to free this woman from the bondage in which satan has held her for 18 years?"

This shamed His enemies, and all the people rejoiced at the wonderful things He had done. I marveled, and couldn't help thinking, *What if I had missed this day? What if I had decided to stay home and rest? What if…What if…What if…? It doesn't matter now. I am whole.* When I saw Him, He set me free!

Points to Ponder

1. Compare this woman's faith to the hopelessness that so many others whom Jesus healed felt. Have you ever experienced such resolute faith? Looking at the woman's example, what can we learn about how to hold onto hope and belief in the midst of difficulty?

2. This woman did not act like a victim. How did that affect her actions? Are there times in your life when despair has kept you "home from the temple"? What might you learn from the woman's testimony?

3. Does the knowledge that Jesus "sees right through you" bring comfort or discomfort? Why?

4. Have you ever been offended (like the synagogue leader) by the way Jesus chose to do something? Does protocol matter to you more than the people involved? What might Jesus have to say about that?

Chapter Twenty-One

Right-Winger
Matthew 12:9-15

I had grown so accustomed to it that I hardly noticed the curious stares from people in the market anymore. The children were the ones I noticed because they were so inquisitive. They would ask questions from a pure heart. "Hey mister, what happened to your hand?" or "Why does your hand look like a prune?" As a young child, those sorts of questions hurt me, but I got used to it, and I realized that people are just curious. They want to hear a story.

Many times I would make up stories to entertain them. "I was walking through the wilderness and was attacked by a lion. As I fought him off, he bit through my arm, and though I was able to kill him with my bare hands, I did lose the use of my right hand." They seldom believed me, but it was a way to break the monotony of the truth; I was born with this dead, withered hand.

It was especially noticeable because every time I was introduced to someone, he would hold out his hand to greet me, and I would have to extend my left hand to his right. That would draw his attention to the useless flesh hanging to my side. I had decided long ago to just live with it, deal with it, get on with my life, so I had.

That is why my date with destiny was such a great day. I was not looking for any change. I had resolved myself to a lifetime without the use of my right hand. I had learned to take care of my necessities with one hand. It is amazing how well you can do without the luxury of an additional hand. I guess it was hard in the beginning, but I had never had the use of it, and so I got along just fine without it. Like I said, I was resolved to the fact that I would always be the way I was—no hope of change, no thought of something different. That was, until I saw Him.

He was different from the other teachers. He would open the books that I had sat and listened to from my youth, but when He taught the words came alive. I began to see things I had never understood before. When He said "The Kingdom of God is here with you," I knew it was so. He would say that the prophets had told of His coming and that He was the One they foretold. I believed! I believed, and He must have known it because every time He came to our town, I would not miss one of His talks. They were encouraging and challenging all at the same time. I didn't miss, and that is why I was there that day.

He was teaching, and several of the older teachers were there too. I was always interested to see them there because they seldom agreed with Jesus' teaching. In fact, they usually got angry and walked out. Why were they so blind to the truth? Jesus had healed people, cast out demons, given sight to the blind, and even made the lame walk again. *Why can't they accept the good Jesus does?* I wondered. I guess jealousy or maybe pride would not allow them to believe the evident truth; Jesus was the Messiah, the Savior, the Promise. Though I knew Jesus had healed others, I was not looking to receive anything. That is part of what makes me so excited about what happened that day.

There I was, hanging out, when Jesus walked up and went into the temple. I knew when He showed up there was going to be food on the table, so to speak. I could not resist going in to listen. When I got inside, I took a seat as close as I could get to Jesus because I did not want to miss a single word. As I was getting settled, in walked the Pharisees and some of the other leaders of that synagogue. I knew we were in store for an awesome time, but I didn't know how radically it would change my life.

I was sitting there waiting for Jesus to begin when I noticed He was looking at the Pharisees in a curious manner. Then, as I thought He was about to approach them with a theological question, He turned to me and said,

"Stand here in the middle of these people where everyone can see you."

I was like a child who had been caught stealing an apple from the market. I froze, acting as if He was talking about the person behind me. But it was apparent to everyone there that He meant me. I stood to my feet and moved to the center of the room. I could not believe He had singled me out of this crowd that had not ceased to grow since I entered the room.

Why Me? I thought. *What can He possibly want me for? Will He embarrass me in front of this whole crowd?* I had become a bit shy and withdrawn to avoid the curiosity of strangers as well as the disingenuous pity from friends and family, so I usually tried to blend into the crowd. *Why has He noticed me? What did I do wrong? Has someone told Him of my failures and sin?* All these questions came to me as I was making my way to the center.

When I got to Him, He addressed the teachers of the law and the Pharisees who were there. "I have a question for you. Is it legal to do good deeds on the Sabbath, or is it a day for doing harm? Is this a day to save life or to destroy it?"

He looked them in the eye, one after another. He seemed angry now. He must have been furious at their hard-nosed religion, and yet the look on His face said He felt very sad because they were stubborn. Then He turned to me and said, "Hold out your hand." I held it out; it was as good as new! *As good as new!* I was beside myself; joy and shock overwhelmed me.

Then the Pharisees called a meeting to plot Jesus' arrest and death. But He knew what they were planning and left the synagogue, and we all followed Him. He healed all the sick who were there, but He cautioned them against spreading the news about His miracles. As we were walking down the street, a demon-possessed man who was both blind and unable to talk was brought to Jesus, and Jesus healed Him so that He could both speak and see. The crowd was amazed. "Maybe Jesus is the Messiah!" they exclaimed.

But when the Pharisees heard about the miracle, their religious feathers were once again ruffled. They were visibly shaken so they puffed up and proclaimed, "He can cast out demons because He is satan, king of devils."

It made me wonder, *Why do religious folks hold God hostage to their experiences rather than taking the miracles as an invitation to know Him more intimately?* I know I'm glad I saw Him and received His kindness and compassion.

Points to Ponder

1. The man wasn't bitter about his deformity, but he wasn't looking for a miracle either. Consider the differences between him and the hunchback woman. What response do you think Jesus wants us to have in such circumstances? Why?

2. The man believed in Jesus even before he was healed. What can you learn from his willingness to trust God even when his life wasn't perfect?

3. Initially, the man was worried that Jesus was going to make a spectacle of him because of his deformity. Instead, Jesus honored him by healing him and made a spectacle of the Pharisees. What does this show you about Jesus' heart for the down-and-out and the outcasts?

4. After the man was healed, he saw several others also receive healing, which only increased his joy. Have you ever struggled to rejoice when others are blessed? Is it hard for you when others receive more attention than you? What issues might Jesus want to address in your heart?

Chapter Twenty-Two

Untouchable

Mark 1:40–45

*H*OW long has it been now? Let me think; when was the last time? Was the last time in anger, or was the last time in love? How long has it been now? When was the last time I was touched by another? Until that special day of all days, when I was touched in a way I never thought possible, it had been a very long time.

The start of each day was the same. Enduring the pain and the shame had become a lifestyle. No one had ever come up with a cure for what I had. Many believed it was a curse from God due to some wrong I had done. Who was I to disagree? I knew myself better than anyone. I had certainly made some mistakes and done some wrongs. *Maybe they are right,* I thought. *Maybe God has indeed decided to make an example out of me to show others what happens when you mess up. But there are many people who have done worse. Why has He chosen to punish me and let others go?*

That's another question you ask when all you can see is yourself and your own plight. One thing was sure, it would not be long until I had no worries at all for little by little every day I was becoming less of a man. Piece by piece I was reducing the space I took up until one day all I would need would be a small hole in the ground to place what was left.

We in the colony would joke about what would be left. Would we wake up one morning to only a head with no body to carry us to our destination? Maybe that's morbid, but it was one of the only ways to laugh, and it seemed to bring some solace. Then the morning would bring another friend's death, the farewell of another "co-condemned."

A touch was so dear to me because I couldn't remember the last time it had happened. The closest I had come to being touched in years was the stones that were thrown toward me. Thrown to say, "You are too close to real people. Get away or you will infect us with your scourge!" *Touching isn't it? Kind of makes you get a lump in your throat, huh?* But I got used to it, and sometimes I would even get close to people just to have some action. We lepers would play a game and take bets as to how close we could come to people before they would throw stones. We had to do something to maintain our sanity.

That was my life since leprosy. Leper was my name, and shame was my game—until that day, until that touch! That day I was walking through the village looking for a hand-out, rummaging through the trash heaps left from the night before, when I heard a crowd approaching. It was unusual for anyone to be out at that time, much less a crowd of that size. What had brought so many out so early? Then I heard someone say, "Jesus, teach us," and another, "Jesus, heal us!"

That one got my attention. *Heal me!* This was Jesus of Nazareth, the prophet who had been teaching and healing all who came to Him. When I saw Him, I ran and fell at His feet. *What will be His response? Will He recoil in horror? Will He throw rocks? Will He kick dirt in my face and yell, "Unclean, Unclean?"* That was the law and the custom of the day. *What will He do? I have to risk it! What other choice do I have?* The way I saw it, there were three doors, death impatiently waiting at one door, agony licking his lips at another, and life standing at the only other door. Which way would I go? It was easy to risk everything when I had nothing to lose. I fell at the feet of potential life and placed myself at His mercy. *What should I say? What do you say to Life when death and agony are chasing you?* "If You want to, You can make me clean," was all I could get out.

Then it happened. He touched me. Not knowing what to expect, I was caught off guard by the soft, gentle touch of His hand. The feeling was so unfamiliar, so foreign, so unbelievable. It was life coursing through me, chasing away death and agony and locking the door behind them. No words had yet been spoken. No miracle of cleansing yet. He had only touched me. You don't know what a touch means until you are deprived of it—no loving touch of a spouse, no cuddling love of a child, not even the slap on the back from a friend. My desire, my longing for just one touch had consumed me at times. And I had been touched. It was better than I had remembered, better than I had dreamed. I could have sat there with His hand on my head forever. Then He said, "I want to cleanse you. Be clean."

Life stopped for a moment as the words seemed to release a flood over my being. I know it was immediate, but it seemed to take hours for the wave of cleansing to roll over me. It was as if I could feel every inch of my body becoming whole. I felt like a wineskin being filled for the first time. Just at the point when I felt like I would burst, I looked and my skin was once again pink with the flow of fresh, clean blood.

The whiteness of leprosy was washed away with the water of His words. The roughness of the scabs and lesions was smooth as a newborn's flesh. The next wave was joy. This was no ripple caused by dropping a stone in a pond. *Tsunami* was a better description—a tidal wave sculpted by the hands of God. I began to shout and praise God, to dance in total abandon, because I was clean. *I am clean!* I could not contain my laughter, "I am clean! Ha, I…I, Ha…He touched me! Ha, Ha, Ha….And oh the joy…oh the flood…Ha, Ha, Ha, Ha, Ha…"

When I got to the end of myself, I saw Him, and when I did, I fell at His feet. He accepted me as I was, but He loved me too much to leave me that way.

Points to Ponder

1. The leper was so focused on his own pain and struggles that he couldn't care about others. Have you ever found yourself in that place? What can (or did) free you to see beyond yourself?

2. The leper had nothing to lose when he fell at Jesus' feet. What about his situation applies to all of us in a spiritual sense? Do any of us really have anything to lose? Explain.

3. Have you ever felt the sort of rejection symbolized by the absence of touch that the leper experienced? What happened?

4. Have you ever experienced spiritual cleansing from Jesus? What did it feel like? What was washed away? Are there areas where you still need to be washed?

Chapter Twenty-Three

Sheepish

Luke 2:8-20

I had wondered for years if it would amount to anything, but after today's events, I knew all that the angels spoke that night had come true. And we were there in the beginning. I was a young lad that night, but I remember it as if it were yesterday.

The air of the Judean spring night was fresh and clean. It flushed impurities of the day from my soul as I breathed. There was a slight chill in the air, just enough to make me wish for the comfort of home and my own bed. But the solace of home and the coziness of my own bed would not be mine that night. I was assigned with my cohorts to watch the flock through the night.

As I stood watch, my mind would wander, asking the deep questions of life like, *Why did I choose this job? Why didn't I leave the family business, go into the city to make a brand new start? Others have done it; why not me? I could make a go of it if I only had the guts to make the move.* I was in the middle of this line of thought when it happened.

A man suddenly appeared in the midst of us; no, no he was an angel, and he looked as if he was on fire. He was shining as bright as the noonday sun. We were shocked and frightened by his appearance. He knew that we were because he said, "Don't be afraid. I'm here to announce a great and joyful event that is meant for everybody, worldwide." Then what he said amazed us even more. "A Savior has just been born in David's town, a Savior who is Messiah and Master. This is what you're to look for: a baby wrapped in a blanket and lying in a manger." As if that wasn't overwhelming enough, just as he finished speaking, the sky was filled with more angels, and they were all praising God and saying, "Glory to God in the heavenly heights. Peace to all men and women on earth who please Him."

As quickly as they had appeared, they vanished, leaving us spinning in the glory of the moment. All of us began talking at the same time, some questioning what had just happened, wondering if they had been dreaming, others accusing the cook of putting something in their soup. As we spoke to one another, we realized that we had all seen the same thing and that we must go and find this baby, this

Savior who is Messiah and Master. The angel had told us what to look for so he must have expected us to go.

It seemed to be a race the way we ran. As we grew close to the town of Bethlehem, my heart was pounding in my chest, not so much from the running as from the excitement of the message. The Savior was born, and I would see Him that night. All the stories about the coming of Messiah were racing through my head, thoughts of the prophecy fulfilled, thoughts of final victory over our enemies, thoughts of David's kingdom restored. All the hopes, all the dreams of ages past, were being fulfilled tonight.

As I approached the hostel where the angel had sent us, I began wondering if we were in the right place. It was the humblest of all the accommodations in the city, if you could call Bethlehem a city. It was the smallest berg around, and it was hardly a place you would go to unless you had family or a special requirement to complete. When we arrived, we were informed that there had indeed been a child born there, but when we were taken to Him, I was shocked even more.

The owner of the place took us to his stable. Surely he was mistaken. We meant a human baby, not a calf or a lamb. Then we walked into the stall where a family was tending the needs of a newborn. Could this be the One the angels were talking about? Could this be the King we had been told would deliver His people? Then we saw Him. There was something about this child. The angel's song was still in our ears as we saw the Promise. With truth confirmed in our hearts, we left proclaiming to all who would listen, the story of the angels, the baby, and the promise fulfilled. It was a time of wonder, a time of glory.

That was over 30 years ago, and I have to admit that I had wondered if it was all true. *Was it merely a memory of a childhood dream, a story told around a campfire?* I had wondered until today. What has cleared away the clouds in my mind? What has happened that could confirm a 33-year-old vision? I saw Him again. No, not the baby, the man, the Savior; I saw the Messiah today.

I had made a trip to Jerusalem because I had heard stories of one who claimed to be the Messiah. I arrived early this morning to find Him, but the high priests and officials of the Romans had crucified Him. It had all happened three days ago. I was preparing to make the return trip when I heard a woman, running through the streets, saying, "He is risen, the Lord is risen."

I could not help it; I had to follow her. Something inside compelled me to go. She arrived at her destination and began beating on the door. When it opened, the people inside seemed shocked by her declaration, and two of them ran out the door and headed toward the tombs. In the confusion, I was able to slip into the room and hear the story that she told. The two who had left returned and confirmed that the tomb where He had been laid was empty. One was full of joy; the other seemed to believe that He had risen, but for some reason, felt no joy in it. *Each of us have our own hidden reasons don't we?* I pondered.

I left there wondering what it all meant. *Could the one they were speaking of be the baby I had seen as a young man? Could He indeed be the Messiah, and could He truly be risen?* In my wondering and questions, I happened to meet the young lady in the market. She was buying food for those in the house, and when I questioned her about the events of the day, she invited me to come back with her and have my questions answered. When we returned, there were several there. They were all talking about the miracle of the resurrection, but one of them said, "I will believe it when I see the scars of the nails in His hands and place my hand in the wound in His side. Then I will believe."

No sooner were the words out of his mouth when the Messiah appeared out of nowhere. All the doors had been locked for fear of the Romans, but He had come in somehow. Standing before us all, He told the one who had doubted, "Happy is anyone who believes without seeing." It was Messiah, the Savior; it was Jesus of Nazareth who had been born in Bethlehem that night over 30 years before.

I had seen Him again. This time there was no doubt about the angel, the promise, or the vision. "Don't be afraid. I'm here to announce a great and joyful event that is meant for everybody, worldwide: A Savior is born… a Savior who is Messiah and Master. Glory to God in the heavenly heights, Peace to all men and women on earth who please Him."

Once again the air of the Judean spring night was fresh and clean. It flushed impurities of the day from my soul as I breathed. There was a slight chill in the air, just enough to make me wish for the comfort of home and my own bed. But the solace of home and the coziness of my own bed would not be mine that night. I would not need them for I would take my comfort from the truth of His resurrection, for I had seen Him in all His glory.

Tomorrow night I will be among the sheep again watching the moonlit sky, waiting, wondering, *Will I see Him again…maybe tonight?*

Points to Ponder

1. Have you ever had to wait a long time to see a promise fulfilled? Did you ever begin to doubt? What happened?

2. When the shepherd doubted, what did he do to revive his faith? How can you revive faith in your life when the promises seem long in coming?

3. Why do you think God chose to announce the birth of the Savior to common shepherds rather than the king or the religious authorities?

4. Why do you think it was important for the shepherds to go see Jesus? What lesson can you glean from this for your own life?

Chapter Twenty-Four

Going Home

Luke 24:13-53

I T was time to go. The events of the last three days had completely drained all strength and energy from us, and we knew we might as well return to our families and our old jobs. There was certainly no future with this group anymore. We not only had seen our leader killed, but now some of the women in the group were saying that they had seen His tomb empty and that two angels had appeared to them and said He had risen. I was not about to hang around a bunch of hysterical women. Some of the disciples went, and they indeed found the tomb empty, but they did not see Jesus. Cleo and I had decided to return to Emmaus so we gathered our belongings and hit the road. Seven miles and we would be home, away from all the confusion and danger in Jerusalem.

As we walked, Cleo and I discussed the events of the last week. "If He would have come into town on a white horse in battle array, He would have been endorsed by the Priests."

"That's ridiculous," stated Cleo. "They were only concerned about losing their power. They were not looking for and didn't want the Messiah to come. That would have eaten into their profits." Cleo was a bit cynical after this past week's events. I had to agree, but we continued to talk about "If onlys" and "what ifs" as if there was any changing the reality. But Jesus was dead, and so was our dream of the restoration of David's kingdom.

As we walked toward home, we were joined by a gentleman heading the same way. He asked what all the discussion was about. What had us so upset and disturbed? When we replied that it was the events from the past week in Jerusalem, He asked, "What events? What happened in Jerusalem?"

This guy has to be new around these parts, I thought. *He acts as if He had never even heard of Jesus.* We described how we had thought Jesus was the Messiah, but now we were saddened by the fact that He was dead and would never fulfill our dreams of a restored kingdom and a free Israel. We also told Him what the women had said and seen.

As we came to the end of our miserable diatribe, the man spoke with a great light in His eyes, "Why can't you simply believe all that the prophets said? Don't you see that these things had to happen, that the Messiah had to suffer and only then enter into His glory?" Then He started at the beginning, with the Books of Moses, and went on through all the Prophets, pointing out everything in the Scriptures that referred to Him. As He spoke, I kept feeling like I would catch on fire from the burning in my heart. The excitement I had felt when Jesus was teaching back on the mountain returned.

When we came to the edge of our city, He acted as if He was going on, but we pressed Him, "Stay and have supper with us. It's nearly evening; the day is done." So He came in with us. He sat down at the table with us, and taking the bread, He blessed and broke and gave it to us. At that moment, open-eyed, wide-eyed, we recognized Him. And then He disappeared.

There was silence in the room for what seemed to be hours. We didn't know what to say. When we did finally speak, we spoke at the same time. Back and forth we talked. "Didn't we feel on fire as He conversed with us on the road, as He opened up the Scriptures for us?"

We didn't waste a minute. We were up and on our way back to Jerusalem. We found the eleven and their friends gathered together, talking away: "It's really happened! The Master has been raised up—Simon saw Him!"

Then we went over everything that had happened on the road and how we recognized Him when He broke the bread. While we were saying all this, Jesus appeared and said, "Peace be with you."

We thought we were seeing a ghost and were scared half to death. He continued, "Don't be upset, and don't let all these doubting questions take over. Look at My hands; look at My feet—it's really Me. Touch Me. Look Me over from head to toe. A ghost doesn't have muscle and bone like this." As He said this, He showed us His hands and feet. We still couldn't believe what we were seeing. It was too much; it seemed too good to be true.

Then He said, "Everything I told you while I was with you comes to this: All the things written about Me in the Law of Moses, in the Prophets, and in the Psalms have to be fulfilled."

He went on to open our understanding of the Word of God, showing us how to read the Law and the Prophets this way. He said, "You can see now how it is written that the Messiah suffers, rises from the dead on the third day, and then a total life-change through the forgiveness of sins is proclaimed in His name to all nations—starting from here, from Jerusalem! You're the first to hear and see it. You're the witnesses. What comes next is very important: I am sending what My Father promised to you, so stay here in the city until He arrives, until you're equipped with power from on high."

He then led us out of the city over to Bethany. Raising His hands, He blessed us, and while He was blessing us, He was carried up to Heaven. We were on our knees, worshiping Him. Then we returned to Jerusalem bursting with joy. We spent all our time in the temple praising God. It was true, and we understood all He had said when we *saw* Him!

Points to Ponder

1. The disciples on the road were trying to figure things out in their minds, but to no avail. Have you ever tried to understand life according to human reasoning? How well did it work?

2. Jesus gave them spiritual understanding. When have you experienced having supernatural understanding from Christ? What difference did it make?

3. Though the two disciples tried to leave everything behind, Jesus sought them out. What does this show you about His heart toward you? How have you experienced Jesus pursuing you?

4. The disciples went from despair to hope and excitement as they began to grasp the full picture of God's plan. What they thought was the end (Jesus' crucifixion), was really the beginning of something much better. When have you been surprised by the plan of God in your life and the way He has used painful or confusing events to bring you to greater things? Explain.

Chapter Twenty-Five

Blueblood

John 4:46-53

L ORD Steward they called me. Sounds impressive enough. Along with all the perks of the office came a certain prestige in the community. Whether it was out of respect or fear, people would bow and scrape to get my business because they knew the credit of Herod Antipas was good. I would pay whatever necessary to get what I wanted. All of the finest things on earth were at my command. I had fine clothes from the most artistic tailors and quality shoes made by the best cobblers, and my chariot was the envy of all who walked the streets of Capernaum. My future was looking so bright I had to squint. But, just when I thought I had it made, the bottom dropped out.

It made no difference that I was a ruler in a most prestigious household. Disease had stricken my little boy. He was going to die. I had spent all my money on physicians who could offer no cure. "Keep him comfortable until the sure end, death," was all they had to offer. This was my boy, my only son, and he was going to die. *Is there nothing I can do? Is there no place I can go to find the answer? Is there no one who can help?* I had prided myself on "making it" in this world. What more could a distant relative to the king hope for. I had all the trappings of royalty. The finances, the appearance, the prestige, made-to-measure clothes, custom-ordered chariots, pure-bred horses to pull them, nothing but the finest—and I would give it all up for a healthy son.

Then I heard about Jesus. He had made a reputation for doing the impossible—changing water to wine, opening blind eyes, healing the crippled, and making withered hands like new. I had even heard about a dead man made alive again. This had to be the answer so I set out to find His whereabouts. I had to act quickly for everyday my son seemed to slip further away into the waiting arms of death. I put out all the feelers I had. Finally I heard He was in Cana, about a good day's trip from Capernaum. The messenger asked if he should leave without delay.

I said, no, I would take care of this myself. No one would be as motivated as me, and besides, what if this Jesus was not inclined to help a courtier in Herod's court? I would have to use all my influence and experience to coerce Him. I left straight away. I had a day's journey. *Will that be longer than my son has?* I was pressed harder by the thought, and my pace increased.

As I pushed the steeds pulling my chariot, pictures of my son at play traveled through my mind. *Why was he the one to be stricken? He was innocent. I am a different matter. I am the one who deserves the malady. Yet my son lies sick unto death, and I am as healthy as a horse. Horse...* "Get up, let's go!" I urged the animals on with a yell and a crack of my whip. I would make it in record time.

I arrived in Cana just before one o'clock, in the heat of the day. As I entered the city, I could see a crowd in the distance. Down the main thoroughfare, I drove my horses at a gallop. Sure enough, there was Jesus. I had never seen Him until now, but I could tell by the crowd and the manner in which He spoke that it was Him. Jumping off of my chariot and pushing through the crowd like some common rabble-rouser, I came face-to-face with Jesus of Nazareth. Without proper introduction, I called out to Him, "Jesus, please come down and heal my son who is on the brink of death!" His next words caught me off guard: "Unless you people are dazzled by a miracle, you refuse to believe."

I was shocked for a moment, but I wouldn't be put off. "Come down! It's life or death for my son."

Instead of rolling His eyes in disgust, Jesus had a glint in His eyes that said He liked my persistence. Jesus simply replied, "Go home. Your son lives."

It was strange for me to be denied my request. It seldom ever happened, considering my status; however, the words seem to carry with them life that transformed my request into a promise. "Go home. Your son lives." *Is that it?* I guess it was enough for me because I believed the bare words Jesus spoke and headed home.

On the road home, I noticed the beauty of the surrounding countryside that had been veiled not only by the blackness of the night, but by the darkness of my soul the day before. I watched the sun set, and the colors seemed to radiate the truth that my son was watching the same. At a slower pace, life can be realized and appreciated. The wind blew a gentle breeze, and the angels sang in harmony with the breeze, "Go home. Your son lives".

I was close to home when some of my servants intercepted me and announced, "Your son lives!" I was glad to hear it, but I already knew it was done and had been since the day before when life poured from Jesus' mouth. With curiosity piqued, I inquired as to what time he began to get better. They said, "The fever broke yesterday afternoon at one o'clock."

That confirmed that the healing had come the very moment Jesus had said, "Your son lives." That clinched it. *Jesus is Messiah.* When I saw Him, I realized that religious knowledge and exercise could never take the place of intimate encounter and relationship.

Points to Ponder

1. The steward of Herod Antipas was used to getting what he wanted. What significance do you see in the fact that Jesus did not go with him (as he asked), but released the healing a different way? How might this apply to your life?

2. His son's illness brought the steward to the end of himself, making him realize that all his wealth and prestige meant nothing to him if his son died. Have you had a similar experience of realizing what really matters to you? What happened?

3. Jesus seemed to like that the steward wouldn't give up, but was tenacious in his asking. What does this teach you about persistence in asking?

4. On his trip to Jesus, the steward did not notice the scenery, but on his way home, his anxiety now replaced with faith, he saw the beauty all around him. What can you learn from this regarding the effect of faith on our perceptions? How have you seen this in your life?

Epilogue

DID you see Him?

He has walked by you with each story you have read. I understand the settings of 2000 years ago are sometimes a bit hard to grasp, but haven't you asked some of those same questions? Did you notice that no matter what the question, the source of the answer was the same—Jesus?

Many years ago another man asked a question that deserved an answer. When God was telling Moses to go and deliver the children of Israel, he asked, "Who shall I say sent me?" God's answer was, "I AM" (see Exod. 3:13-14). It seems like a strange answer until you think about it. What do you have need of? The answer is I AM. I AM, period. It made no difference what Moses needed; God was the I AM. God says, "I AM the one who parts your Red Sea. I AM water in the desert. I AM bread when you are hungry. I AM a healing salve when you are injured! I AM! Period."

Jesus is the I AM in every situation. What did the leper need? Jesus was healing and salvation. What did Peter need? Jesus was restoration of relationship. Jesus is still the I AM. What do you need? Jesus is your I AM if you will see Him for who He is. Will you see Him, or will you let pride keep you from running to Him until it is too late? Will you see Him, or will you allow the circumstances to blind you to the truth? Will you see Him, or will you consider yourself unworthy?

You may be saying, "Randy, I would like to see Him. I just can't take that step. I don't know what to do or how to do it. If I could see Him, I would believe." Perhaps you are one of those who think "seeing is believing." Let me tell you something that may clear this up for you. Following Christ is a lot like using a flashlight in the dark. You turn on the flashlight, and you just see the next step. As you step out and move toward the light, you are able to see the next step. It is like that with the Lord. Believe that He will show the next step and take the first one.

Step toward the light in the light you have. You see Jesus when you move toward Him, and you do this through faith. You see, *believing is seeing!* If you believe, you will see. If you see Him, you see the answer. He is your I AM! Jesus, the I

AM, can change your now and your eternity when you *see* Him!

If you are sitting there and wondering *What now,* you must make it final. You can ensure that you will see Him. It is simple, but it isn't easy. If you want to, you can pray. Talk to God like you would your best friend; say this simple prayer, and let Jesus Christ, the one who died for you, take control of your life and make you what He designed you to be.

Why don't you say something like:

God, I need to see with new eyes. I need to give You control, and so right now, as much as I know how, I give You my life. Give me what I need to believe so that I might see You. Jesus, please take over as my Boss, as my CEO, as my Lord. I don't understand all that means, but I trust You to show me all I need and all I am to be for You. Thank You for dying for me and paying the debt I owed. I trust You to save me and form me into the purpose You created me for. Here's my life, such as it is. In Your name I pray, amen!

Here's one more promise before we finish. First John 3 says,

Behold what manner of love the Father has bestowed on us, that we should be called children of God! Therefore the world does not know us, because it did not know Him. Beloved, now we are children of God; and it has

not yet been revealed what we shall be, but we know that when He is revealed, we shall be like Him, for we shall see Him as He is (1 John 3:1-2).

As you grow in relationship with Jesus, He will reveal more of Himself to you. As He does, when you see Him, you will become like Him more and more until the day of His return. And that my friend, will be the time when we see Him together.

Blessings! We will see you again soon.

About Randy Hill

In 35 years of ministry, Randy Hill has worn many hats and seen many facets of ministry. His ministry began at the age of 15 when he purchased a public address system and began traveling across the West Texas Plains singing and preaching. His travels eventually led him to Asia, Europe, and Russia.

While building homes in Lubbock, Randy answered the call to full-time ministry and moved to the Dallas area to serve a new church as an associate pastor. He invested 17 years as Associate Pastor of Christ Our King Community Church in Plano, Texas. The church was a one-year-old work when he and his wife arrived to help. They have been involved in every area of ministry from mopping floors to preaching the Word. "It has been a long 25 and a short 25 years," Randy says. "If I had known what was in store for us when I came, I would have stayed in the building business, but after going through what was definitely God's plan, I would not have had it any other way. I guess that is the reason God only shows us one step at a time."

Randy has been the Children's Pastor, Music Pastor, Church Administrator, Associate Pastor, and Chief cook and bottle washer. This history has given him a different perspective on a lot of things. In 1996 Randy felt God calling once again. This call was to plant a new church. At that time Randy was the owner of a local business and felt he would have to sell it to answer the call. Plans were laid and the business sold.

Presently He is the senior leader at Summit Church. Randy says, "Our mission as a church is REVIVAL and can be summed up in one thing that Jesus said, 'Your kingdom come, Your will be done, on earth as it is in Heaven.' The Summit is a place where the hurting, helpless, and hopeless can find healing, help, and hope in Jesus Christ!"

IN THE RIGHT HANDS, THIS BOOK WILL CHANGE LIVES!

Most of the people who need this message will not be looking for this book. To change their lives, you need to put a copy of this book in their hands.

> *But others (seeds) fell into good ground, and brought forth fruit, some a hundred-fold, some sixty-fold, some thirty-fold* (Matthew 13:8).

Our ministry is constantly seeking methods to find the good ground, the people who need this anointed message to change their lives. Will you help us reach these people?

> *Remember this—a farmer who plants only a few seeds will get a small crop. But the one who plants generously will get a generous crop* (2 Corinthians 9:6).

EXTEND THIS MINISTRY BY SOWING
3 BOOKS, 5 BOOKS, 10 BOOKS, **OR MORE TODAY,** AND BECOME A LIFE CHANGER!

Thank you,

Don Nori Sr., Founder
Destiny Image
Since 1982

DESTINY IMAGE PUBLISHERS, INC.

*"Speaking to the Purposes of God for This Generation
and for the Generations to Come."*

VISIT OUR NEW SITE HOME AT
WWW.DESTINYIMAGE.COM

FREE SUBSCRIPTION TO DI NEWSLETTER

Receive free unpublished articles by top DI authors, exclusive

discounts, and free downloads from our best and newest books.

Visit www.destinyimage.com to subscribe.

Write to: Destiny Image
               P.O. Box 310
               Shippensburg, PA 17257-0310

Call: 1-800-722-6774

Email: orders@destinyimage.com

For a complete list of our titles or to place an order
online, visit www.destinyimage.com.

FIND US ON FACEBOOK OR FOLLOW US ON TWITTER.

www.facebook.com/destinyimage   facebook
www.twitter.com/destinyimage   twitter

—